INSTRUCTION BOOK FOR

BEGINNING ORGANISTS

DAVID N. JOHNSON

AUGSBURG PUBLISHING HOUSE

Instruction Book for Beginning Organists

Manufactured in the United States of America

Preface

This Instruction Book is designed for beginning church organists. The emphasis throughout the book is practical, although some chapters deal with basic theoretical concepts.

Normally, the prerequisite for organ study is a number of years of piano instruction. It is difficult to say precisely how many years of piano lessons should be required, since the rate of learning or accomplishment varies widely among individuals. An evaluation of the achievements of the student is a more reliable index of proficiency than the number of years of study. A piano student who has achieved some technical and artistic mastery of representative compositions by J. S. Bach, Haydn, Mozart or Beethoven, Chopin, and a few contemporary composers, should be considered ready for organ lessons.

Depending on the needs of the individual students, the instructor should feel free to alter the indicated sequence of chapters in this manual, to omit various sections, or to start several chapters simultaneously. Such a flexibility of approach takes into account the wide variety of backgrounds, skills, and weaknesses to be found among students.

Second Printing 1965

Contents

CHAPTER   PAGE

1   Introduction to the Instrument 1

2   The Pedals 5

3   The Manuals: Legato 18

4   Practice Habits 32

5   The Pedals: Heel and Toe 34

6   Phrasing 39

7   Pedal Phrasing and Additional Aspects of Pedal Technique 42

8   Co-ordination 47

9   Trios 60

10   Alternate Toes 77

11   Repeated Notes 79

12   The Manuals: Repeated Notes and Voice Leading 82

13   Three Special Problems in Voice Leading 95

14   Co-ordination: Repeated Notes 97

15   The Hymn 106

16   The Hymn: Free Harmonizations 130

17   Stops and Registration 149

18   Ornamentation 156

19   Legato and Staccato Styles 159

20   The Organist in Church Work; Service Playing 160

21   Playing on Two Manuals with One Hand 162

22   Improvisation for the Beginner 167

23   Left Hand Carrying Three Legato Voices 172

24   On Teaching 178

Chapter One

Introduction to the Instrument

The student should be seated at about the midpoint of the bench, far enough forward, or back, so that both hands and feet may be lifted without a feeling of imbalance. The height of most organ benches is adjustable. A little experimentation will help determine what bench height causes the least fatigue and is most suitable for efficiency in playing and reaching the pedals.

The distance from the bench to the keys is also adjustable. The bench should be just close enough so that the hands can reach all the manuals, or shift between them quickly, without placing a strain on the back. As to the pedals, if the bench is too far forward or back, leg muscles will quickly become tired and uncomfortable.

The student may pivot somewhat as he sits on the bench, but should avoid sliding back and forth to reach high and low pedal notes. Posture should be comfortable and relaxed. Later, if the student seems to be developing a poor habit, such as exaggerated arm and elbow motion, the instructor may call it to his attention. However, too much emphasis upon a rigid "proper" posture at first can lead to an attitude of discomfort on the part of the student, drawing attention away from the mechanics and artistry of making music.

While organs in most small churches have two manuals, many somewhat larger instruments have three or more, up to five, six, or even seven manuals. The purposes of several keyboards (including the pedal board, which is an additional keyboard) are to provide flexibility, variety, and maneuverability, as well as utilization of the feet to perform a separate musical line. Both hands may be on any one manual, or the left hand may be on one while the right hand is on another, or they may move quickly back and forth, in concerto style, from one manual to another. There is no rule that the left hand must be on the lower manual, as accompaniment, while the right hand is on the upper manual; nor is one manual limited exclusively to solo sounds. It is true, however, that the different manuals have somewhat different purposes and, consequently, somewhat different stops and tonal features. Although the role of the pedal is normally to provide bass tones, it is sometimes required to play a soprano melody, above the pitch of the manuals; and on most organs stops are provided for pedal pitch flexibility.

At the first lesson the instructor may discuss proper care of the instrument, including any special precautions or maintenance procedures peculiar to the local church. Because of temperature differentials, it is advisable to leave the swell shades open when the organ is not in use. All stops should be cancelled when the organ is turned off; the crescendo pedal or sforzando pedal must never be left on when the organ is turned off.

It should be pointed out that normal, proper practice does an organ no harm, whether it be large or small. Indeed, the organ, being essentially a mechanical instrument, suffers most from inactivity. It is best for the average church organ to be used at least one hour a day. Adequate usage keeps the leathers limber and small parts free of dust. Given a good, heavy-duty blower, an organ can be played eight or more hours per day without harm. By the same token, loud playing does not damage the instrument or cause excessive wear.

After the preliminaries have been covered, the student is ready to investigate sounds on the instrument. It will first be noted that if there are no stops on, there is no sound when a key is depressed. This fact is significant: it is up to the organist, more than any other instrumentalist, to construct his own world of tone and sound, by proper selection of stops.

Next, using an 8' stop, the student should play a few manual chords. Some differences from piano style and technique will be observed:

1. Whether the attack is swift or slow, heavy or gentle, loudness remains the same (similarly, if one presses very hard in turning on a light switch, he does not get a brighter light). Tone is unaffected by weight of touch; and, except for tracker or mechanical action, it is not affected by speed of attack.
2. As long as the key is depressed, the tone remains constant and does not die away. On the other hand, the tone ceases, except for building reverberation, immediately upon release of the key, since there is no sustaining pedal. In organ playing, therefore, proper timing of release of keys is virtually as important as attack.
3. The organist builds his own pitches, volume, and tone quality.

The student should next hold a chord, or a pedal key, and hear each stop individually throughout the entire organ. This orientation process reveals (1) the location of stops which control the different keyboards, (2) the non-speaking stops such as couplers and tremulant, and (3) the wide variety of pitches and timbres available. Each speaking stop has a name and either an Arabic number or a Roman numeral. The name refers to the tone color or timbre, and the number refers to the pitch or pitches at which the stop speaks.

The standard American organ console has 61 keys to each manual (compass, CC to c^4)* and 32 pedal keys (compass, CCC to G with a reference point of 16'; or CC to g^1 at 8'). On the manuals, Middle C is the third C from the bottom or the fourth C from the top of the keyboard. On the pedals, Middle C at 8' is not in the middle range of the pedalboard, but is the highest C in the upper range of the board. In other words, the manuals and the pedals begin with the same note (CC at 8').

In order to determine the meaning of the figures on the speaking stops, and the specific pitches which they control, hold Middle C on one of the manuals. Putting on an 8' stop on that manual will produce the tone Middle C; the same holds true in the pedal division. This is true of all 8' stops, which speak at "normal" or "piano" or "concert" pitch. Experimentation with other stops will demonstrate that 4' stops speak one octave high, 2' stops speak two octaves high, and so forth. The following table will illustrate:

At Middle C	range	tone sounding
8'	unison	c^1
4'	one octave higher	c^2
2 2/3'	one octave plus a perfect fifth higher	g^2
2'	two octaves higher	c^3
1 3/5'	two octaves plus a major third higher	e^3
1 1/3'	two octaves plus a perfect fifth higher	g^3
1'	three octaves higher	c^4
32'	two octaves lower	CC
16'	one octave lower	C
10 2/3'	one perfect fourth lower	G
5 1/3'	one perfect fifth higher	g^1
3 1/5'	one octave plus a major third higher	e^2

This table is incomplete, since it does not include the Septiemes (such as 1 1/7') and some other rare pitches.

This wide variety of pitches is made available to the organist in order that many possibilities be provided for richness of tone, volume, weight, brilliance, and tonal coloration (such as reediness).

These particular pitches are made available to the organist for the following reason: they are all component members of the harmonic series or overtone structure of musical tones. They are therefore the elements—or building blocks—which go into the creation of various complex musical sounds.

The figure "8" has been chosen to signify unison pitch because the length of the longest, and therefore the lowest, pipe of a rank of pipes is approximately eight feet ("rank" is the term used for a row of pipes voiced as a unit and controlled by a stop); it is convenient to label a rank of pipes according to the longest pipe to be found in that rank. There are certain exceptions to this rule: stopped pipes

---

*No uniform practice exists regarding the method of indicating different octaves. The system used here (c^1 as middle c) seems preferred by organ builders.

speak approximately one octave lower than open pipes, and the lengths of reed resonators vary widely; therefore the custom has arisen of using the number which applies to the "sound" length of a pipe (that is, the tone it sounds, or the note it plays) rather than the physical length of the pipe. It should be observed that the convention of applying the symbol "8'" to unison organ stops will be found virtually all over the world; this fact is convenient when one visits a strange organ.

A Roman numeral on a stop indicates the number of ranks brought into play by drawing that stop. For example, "III" signifies that three pipes will speak when the performer depresses one key, such as Middle C. These stops are usually "mixtures," but the name of the stop may not necessarily be Mixture. They usually feature high-pitched pipes, but do not remain at the same relative pitch throughout their register, but break back. Therefore a mixture imparts a differing quality to a combination in lower and higher registers. This effect results in clarity in contrapuntal music, and brilliance, sheen, and grandeur in homophonic passages. The number of ranks in a mixture varies from II to VII or more. Certain stops with Roman numerals, such as Sesquialtera II, and Grand Cornet X (32'), are special-purpose stops rather than mixtures in the strict sense of the word.

In addition to its number, each speaking stop also has a name, which is intended by the builder to indicate its timbre, or construction, or tonal characteristics. Unfortunately, while builders can be depended upon to use stop numerals in accepted standard ways, there is an extremely wide variance in usage of descriptive names and terminologies of tone quality. It is therefore difficult to predict the precise sound of a stop by its name, although familiarity with the work of the builder will help. The best way for the beginner to learn stop names and their meanings is simply to listen to sounds and associate them with stop names on as many different organs as possible. It must be understood that, unlike pianos, all of which have similar tonal features, most organs are somewhat different. This difference is partly due to the fact that acoustics of a building affect the sound of an organ, and the organ and its room interact to become one musical instrument. Furthermore, most organ builders do not deliver the same package of identical components to all buyers. Rather, almost every organ is custom built for the persons who will play it, those who will hear it, and perhaps sing to it, and the individual and unique purposes for which it is intended. The student will therefore discover that if he practices on several instruments not only will the total effect of the ensembles be different, but also individual stops with the same names may not be identical.

Most organs are equipped with couplers. These are not speaking stops, but rather have the purpose of linking together different keyboards at various pitches, enabling the performer to draw into use stops on one manual while playing on another or the pedals. Couplers greatly increase the flexibility and tonal possibilities of the average organ, although when used to excess they tend to destroy the individual tonal integrity of the various divisions of the instrument. In some very large installations their use is somewhat unnecessary. A demonstration by the instructor can make their use quite clear.

The matter of speed is a problem to many beginning organ students. Coming directly from piano study, some assume that organ and piano tempi are identical. But this is not quite the case. The style of the organ tends more to feature nobility and grandeur than dazzling pyrotechnics; and where an increase of tempo in piano playing may lead to excitement, a corresponding increase in organ playing often cheapens the music, decreasing its aesthetic content and meaning. There are exceptions, and an occasional brilliant organ *prestissimo* can be overpoweringly impressive; but the student should not think of organ sixteenth notes in the same artistic way as those which occur in piano *allegro* and *vivace* passages. Furthermore, large buildings tend to have long reverberation periods, sometimes amounting to four or six seconds or more. Under such circumstances slower tempi are required, for the sake of clarity.

The characteristic organ style, which should become the student's normal touch, is legato. A succession of tones should not be detached unless there is an artistic reason for so doing.

Which stops should be used by the beginner, and how many? Should the hands be on separate manuals, and should the pedals be used all the time? Here are a few brief generalities on registration:

1. The music will usually indicate clearly whether or not pedal is to be used. If there are no indications, but the score consists of three lines, or staves, the top staff is taken by the right hand, the middle by the left, and the lower by the pedals. Use of pedals in hymns will be treated later.
2. Unless the music carries specific instructions to the contrary, 8' should always be used as the basic manual pitch and 16' as the basic pedal pitch. This procedure causes the pedals to sound one octave lower than written, which is intended by organ composers. As a general rule, the pedal combination should also contain

an 8′ stop for pitch clarity and definition. In trying to arrive at suitable manual combinations, the best thing to do as a normal procedure is to select one 8′ stop, then add to it a 4′ and perhaps additional upper work, until the desired result is obtained. Usually one 8′ stop of the right tone color is sufficient. Addition of many 8′ stops can result in undesirable thickness and blurred lines. The fewer stops of lower pitch used, the more clarity, vitality, and energy achieved. Similarly, when volume is desired, one may utilize the louder 8′ stops, while at the same time leaving off the softer 8′ ranks. The amateur often draws a multitude of stops, laboring under the misconception that bigger, better sound is achieved by more ranks. But builders do not design organs on this additive principle. Rather, certain groups of stops, often of different pitches, are designed to go together for greater volume, and other stops are for different purposes. In regard to the pedals, they should be loud and clear enough so that pitch can be distinctly heard. This does not necessarily mean a combination of several loud 16′ stops. Rather, "loudness"— which, according to acousticians and engineers is a somewhat subjective term—is often best obtained by one 16′ stop, one 8′ stop, and several higher pitches.

3. If the manual parts contain chords, both hands are normally played on one manual. If the two hands are assigned three parts, such as soprano, alto, and tenor, and the alto is transferred occasionally between the hands, all three parts should be played on one manual. Otherwise, if the soprano is isolated on a special solo manual, the alto may become illogically and arbitrarily prominent when the right hand is required to carry it on the solo manual.

4. If the right hand carries a theme, or an obviously prominent melody, and is not responsible for additional voices at any time, it may be appropriately played on a separate manual featuring a distinct solo stop or solo combination. The left hand then carries more quiet accompanimental voices. In order to preserve the solo qualities of the right hand in this case, and in order to provide maximum tonal contrast between the manuals, care should be taken to avoid using the featured solo timbre in the accompaniment. In other words, if flutes are selected for the solo, the left hand accompaniment should consist of strings or soft principals. Furthermore, one should normally try to avoid the same or similar pitch spectra in both solo and accompaniment. For example, if the solo consists of flutes 8′, 4′, 2 2/3′ and 2′, the student should avoid using an accompaniment consisting of 8′ and 2′, or 8′, 4′ and 2′. Similar pitch bands should be used only when homogeneity of voices is a goal (of course this does not apply when both solo and accompaniment consist of a single 8′ stop each).

5. Similarly, if the left hand carries a single-voice theme, it may appropriately be played on a separate solo manual.

6. When the music is a trio, and right and left hand carry contrapuntal melodies of equal prominent and thematic significance, two combinations, somewhat different in both timbre (at least at the 8′ level) and pitch band, but about equivalent in volume, should be selected for the manuals, together with a complementary pedal.

Chapter Two

The Pedals

The student's shoes should have soles of medium thickness (not rubber), a normal indentation or "cut" in front of the heels, and moderately thick heels (rubber or leather, at the preference of the student). If the shoe is perfectly flat from tip of toe to heel, without heel notch or cut, it is difficult to play passages which require alternation of heel and toe. If the sole is too thick, the foot loses sensitivity of contact with the keys. If the sole is too thin, the foot muscles do unnecessary work and tire easily. If the sole is rubber, sliding, dexterity, and speed are hindered. Some prefer a rubber heel for gripping and pivoting; others prefer a leather heel for maneuverability. American girls ordinarily avoid high heels with little contact area, although it should be noted that some of the French women virtuosi wear extremely high heels.

The instructor may wish to begin this chapter with a demonstration of three or four hymns, to show actual pedal technique in operation.

The first and basic problem for the student is how to find the pedal keys without looking at the feet. Under normal conditions the eyes simply do not have an opportunity to glance down at the pedals. Several methods have been developed for finding the pedal keys.

1. The interval method, or "gap system," in which the student first locates, with his toe, a space where there is no black key (between E-F and B-c^1) and then, having determined his location, proceeds up or down to the desired note by counting the keys as he glides over them. The gaps are found either by moving along the white keys with the tip of the toe in contact with the tip of the black keys until the gap is encountered, or by sliding along the tops of the black keys about one inch from the front tips until the absence of a black key indicates E-F or B-c^1.

2. The central reference location system, in which two keys, C for the left foot and E for the right foot, are always used as starting points. Keys are found and intervals learned by gliding over one, two, or more keys, and the performer always keeps in mind the interval between the last key played by one foot and the next to be played by that same foot.

3. The kinesthetic sensation method, which is based on the physiological fact that sensations from nerve endings in muscles and joints give rise to perception of movement and position. In other words, by the internal "feel" of a person's leg, ankle, and foot, he knows approximately where it is poised. The performer always sits over the key D, and finds all keys kinesthetically.

4. The toe-heels-toe "angle" or "span" method: The knees are kept together. With heels touching, the toes may spread apart as much as a fifth. Relative angles and the sizes of various intervals are learned by habit and practice; the feet work together, proceeding sideways, crab-like, along the white keys. (Beyond the interval of an octave, the knees are not kept touching.)

For beginners, the gap system is most accurate. It is not difficult and it may be learned quickly. However, its disadvantage is that it is somewhat less maneuverable in fast passages. Although the elementary pedal exercises in this method follow the gap system, there is utilization of the central reference system and the toe-heels-toe span method as the student progresses. In actual practice, students usually discover that after a time they are also using the kinesthetic method somewhat, knowing instinctively by muscle perception the locations of some of the keys. This shift of technique, which is evidently normal, does no harm; indeed, some instructors advocate use of different systems of pedaling for pedal passages of varying characteristics.

It is suggested that the student observe the following instructions closely.

On the standard 32-note pedal board, the five gaps are designated as follows: EE-FF; BB-C; E-F; B-c¹; and e¹-f¹. First, set up a pedal stop combination of at least 16', 8', and 4', *mf*. Look at the pedals just long enough to place the left toe in the BB-C gap; then avoid looking at the pedals again until told to do so. The right foot may rest on the swell pedal or, if there is a rail or bottom board on the organ bench, rest upon it. Next, play the following notes with the left toe. *Note:* in the case of men's somewhat wider shoes, play with either the left or right side of the sole, whichever is easier and most convenient, near the toe, turning the foot slightly as necessary; all this area is called the "toe."

Next, without looking at the pedals, glide out of the BB-C gap. With the tip of your toe maintaining continual contact with the tip of the black keys, slide on the tops of the white keys up to the next gap, E-F. Play the following notes:

Next, glide down the pedal board past the BB-C gap to the EE-FF gap and play the following notes:

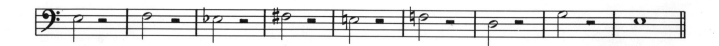

Next, looking at the pedals for a moment, place your left foot out of the way and position your right foot in the E-F gap. Then, avoid looking at the pedals as you play the following notes:

Gliding down the white keys, but always maintaining contact with the tips of the black keys, locate BB-C (still with the right foot), and play the following:

Then proceed up to the proper gap and play:

The following standard symbols are used:

∧ (below the staff) left toe

⌢ ⤢ (below the staff) left heel

∧ (above the staff) right toe

∪ (above the staff) right heel

When using the toe, pivot the foot from the ankle as much as you can, rather than moving the entire leg and knee up and down. When using the heel, there will, of necessity, be more leg movement.

After the preliminary discovery exercises outlined above have been played two or three times, the student is ready to start practicing the pedal exercises below. Some metronome markings are given. The student should obtain a metronome, since its use is essential to the cultivation of good organ style and technique. The metronome assists in the mastery of rhythmic accuracy and provides a check on tempo. However, the student must not become so addicted to dependence upon the metronome that he fails to develop a strong inner sense of rhythmic vitality and metric accuracy. Therefore the metronome is indispensable for some kinds of practice but should not be used always or to excess.

About every tenth exercise, even including the most elementary studies, should be memorized by the student. Memorization is excellent training, because it frees the performer from helpless dependence upon the printed page, thus enabling him to devote greater attention to musical matters; because it forces him to master technical problems more competently, and thus play with solid mechanical assurance; and because it leads him to more careful musical analysis of the composition, which in turn usually leads to a more artistic performance. Although church services are not usually played from memory, organists should memorize compositions for other public performances. The student will find that he memorizes organ works much more easily and readily after a solid background of piano memorization. It is not necessary for the instructor to have had any memorization experience or training in order that memorization assignments be given to the student.

The following exercises are for pedals alone. Toes only should be used until use of the heel is specified. It is suggested that a stop combination of 16', 8', and 4', *mf*, be used for all these exercises, except as occasionally noted (the instructor may, however, wish to recommend that the student use only 8' and 2', or 4' and 2' combinations if difficulty is encountered in achieving clarity). The student should remember to practice for precision of release, as well as attack.

1 **Left foot**
   Begin at *andante* (♩=76); increase tempo gradually to *allegro* (♩=144)

2 Right foot
(Begin at ♩ = 76; increase gradually to ♩ = 144)

3 Alternate toes
Legato. Begin at *adagio* (♩=60); increase tempo gradually to *vivace* (♩ =184). Synchronize release of one note precisely with attack of the next.

4 Left foot
Allegretto. The BB-C and E-F gaps with one foot

5 Right foot

6 Toes only, both feet
Larghetto (♩=76). Practice for rhythmic precision of the dotted quarter plus eighth pattern.

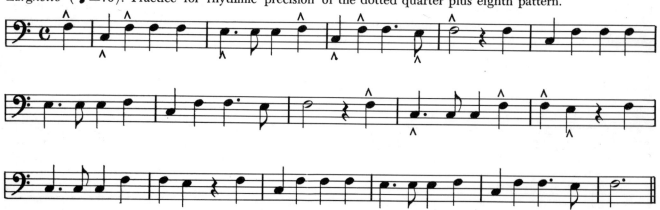

7 Alternate toes on one key.
Andante

8 Alternate toes
Work toward tempo of *allegro* (♩=144).
Practice for accuracy at increased speeds.

9 Left foot only
Andante. Widening range through additional gaps

10 Right foot only
Additional gaps

*Give this measure exactly three beats (count six quarter notes) and do not cut it short. Cultivate the habit, even in simple exercises, of playing with rhythmic accuracy and precision regardless of the "activity"—or lack of it—in a measure. It is a complete misconception for the student to think he must apologize for a measure in which "nothing seems to be happening" musically, by hurrying on too quickly to the next downbeat. The phrase endings and momentary pauses which occur in music are of artistic consequence and must not be mutilated.

11 Alternate toes
Moderato
Additional gaps

12 Alternate toes
Allegro

13 Alternate toes
Vivace

14 *Allegretto*

15 Left foot, toe only
Allegro moderato. Introduction to the black keys. Observe rests carefully, releasing with precision; pivot from the ankle without excess leg motion.

10

16 Right foot, toe only
Andante

17 Left toe
Drill for A♭

18 Right toe
Drill for A♭

19 Black keys, alternate toes
Legato, poco andante (♩=88).

20 *Allegro molto (♩=132; increase to ♩.=100)*

21 Legato and detached combinations
(♩=54 to 96)

22 Left toe
Moderato. Combinations of black and white keys

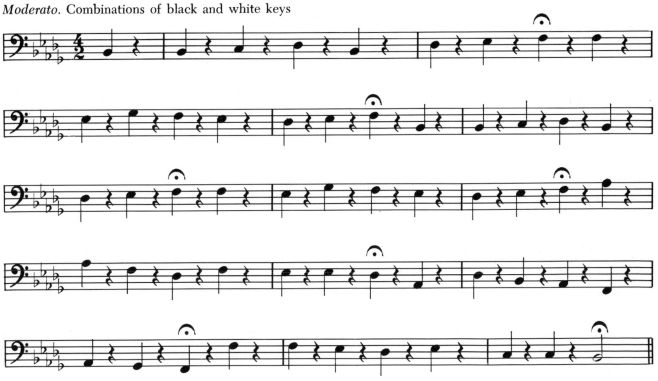

23 Right toe
Moderato

24 Black and white keys, alternate toes
(♩=88). *mp*, 8′ and 4′ only

25 *Quasi Presto. ff*, 16′, 8′, 4′, 2′ and mixtures

26 Alternate toes on one note, *staccato.*
Allegro molto. Be sure detached notes are even, and intervals between notes are of equal length.

27 Left toe. White key drill
Andante. mf, 8′, 4′, and 2′

28 Right toe. White key drill
Moderato. mf, 8′, 4′, and 2′

29 Alternate toes
Adagio (♩=76). Lyrical, mp, 8′ and 2′ only

30 Drill for rhythmic accuracy and precision.
Larghetto (♩=69)

31 Changes of metre and tempo
Moderato (♩=104)

Vivace Molto (♩.=84)

poco rit.

Tempo I

16

32 *Presto* (♪=152 to ♩.=63)
ff, 16′, 8′, 4′ Principals and Reeds with mixtures.

33 *Moderato* (♩.=54). *mp*, 16′, 8′, and 4′
Maintain steady tempo and avoid hurrying a long series of triplets.

34 *Allegro moderato*

17

Chapter Three

The Manuals: Legato

The normal style of organ playing, as mentioned before, is legato. The skill of connecting two notes smoothly must be mastered from the beginning.

As a preliminary exercise, practice major and harmonic minor scales one octave, ascending and descending, hands separately and then together. Concentrate: be continually aware that your purpose in this drill is to connect notes properly.

Andante. mf, Great, 8′, 4′, and 2′

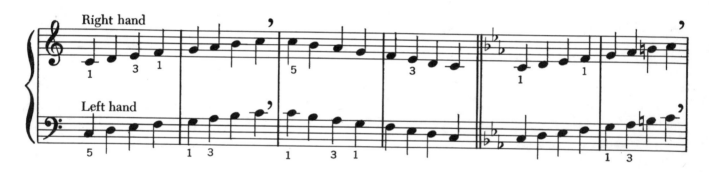

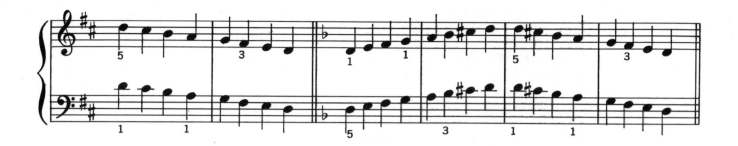

Continue through all scales as outlined above. But notice that, after this preliminary exercise, it is rarely necessary to practice manual scales on the organ: piano touch, because of its resistance, is usually considered better for scale practice.

Often, when one hand is carrying two or three voices, various procedures, such as substitution, crossing third or fourth finger over fifth finger, thumb glissando, and black key to white key slide or glissando, must be employed, in order to achieve complete legato.

Substitution, or changing fingers on one key, is a common occurrence and must be practiced thoroughly. As a preparatory study, practice the following one-voice exercises. Make the finger substitution early in the duration of the note.

Right hand
Andante. mp, Swell, 8′ and 4′

Left hand

1   2-1   2-1   2-1   2   1-2   1-2   1-2   1   2   3-2   3-2   3-2   3   2-3   2-3   2-3   2

3   4-3   4-3   4-3   4   3-4   3-4   3-4   3   4   5-4   5-4   5-4   5   4-5   4-5   4-5   4

2   1-2   1-2   1-2   1   2-1   2-1   2-1   2   3   2-3   2-3   2-3   2   3-2   3-2   3-2   3

4   3-4   3-4   3-4   3   4-3   4-3   4-3   4   5   4-5   4-5   4-5   4   5-4   5-4   5-4   5

Right hand. One hand carrying two voices.

Left hand

Right hand. Drill in crossing 4th finger over 5th.

Right hand. 3rd and 5th finger drill.

Left hand. 4th and 5th finger drill.

Left hand. 3rd and 5th finger drill.

The slide, or glissando
Right hand. *Allegretto*. Black key to white key, Legato, on one finger.

Practice the above exercise with the left hand one octave lower, using finger glissandi.

Thumb slide, or glissando
Right hand, thumb only, Legato. Utilize base or tip of the thumb, as appropriate. When necessary, change between base and tip of the thumb on the same key.
4′ Spitzflöte only.

Left hand, thumb only
Legato, except as rests are indicated. *p*, 8′ and 2′

22

The following exercises will indicate various aspects of the problem of maintaining independence of voices. From the beginning, the student must learn the concept of independent voice leading: direction, movement, phrasing, and rests in one line must not influence or affect any other voices being carried by the same hand.

1 Right hand only

Adagio, molto legato. Swell or Great, *mp,* 8′ and 4′

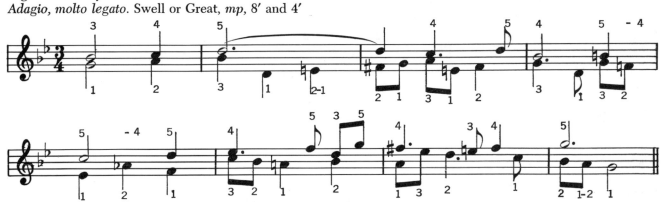

Suggestions to the student: at all times during the exercise above, be certain that you are playing two notes, and neither more nor less than two. Do not insert any rests or phrasing. Specifically guard against the following typical errors:

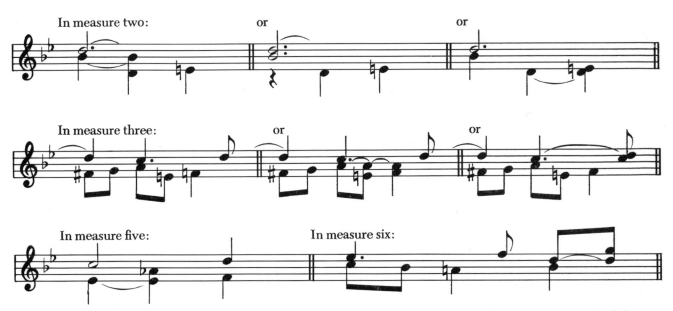

Always think of each voice as a separate and independent entity. Do not hold over one note while the same voice moves to its next note—just as the human voice cannot sing two notes at a time.

Note: fingerings indicated in this method are suggestions only and should not be considered the only possibilities. Because of individual differences in size of hand, the student should refinger exercises when necessary.

2 Right hand

3 Right hand
Andante

Guard against the following errors in measure one:

4 Left hand
Andante, molto legato. Swell or Great, *mp*, 8′ and 4′

24

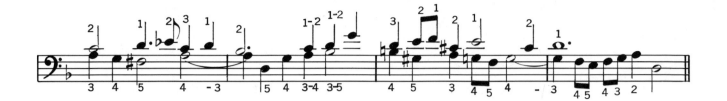

5 Left hand
Moderato

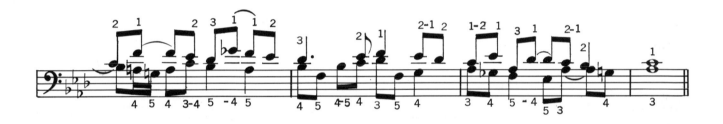

6 Left hand
Adagio, quasi andante

7 Right hand
Andantino. Rests in two-voice designs: legato except as rests occur

8 Right hand
Allegretto. Note: be sure to hold D♭ quarter note in measure four its full value.

9 Left hand
The two time signatures indicate that two metres will be found, but not necessarily in alternate measures, in this exercise.

10 Left hand

Andante con moto. The student should begin to work out his own fingerings.

In the following exercises one hand carries three voices.

11 Right hand
Largo. p to mp

12 Right hand
Larghetto

13 Right hand
Andante

14 Left hand
Adagio

15 Left hand
Moderato

16 Left hand
Andante

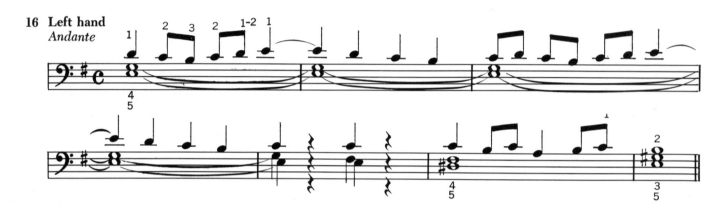

17 Right hand

18 Right hand

19 Right hand

20 Left hand

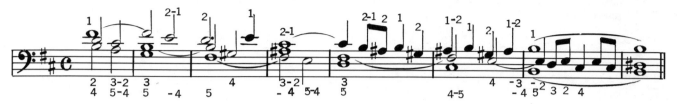

21 Left hand

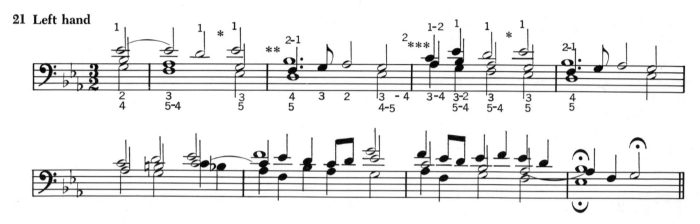

*The thumb cannot connect D and E♭ here; therefore it is not possible to maintain a complete legato. Keep the gap of silence between the two notes to a minimum by moving the thumb as rapidly as possible at the third beat. (Observe that the B♭ at **, being a dotted whole note, is held throughout the measure; the tenor then proceeds legato to C.)

The A♭ at ***, having double stems, carries both baritone and bass voices.

22 Left hand

The following exercises provide drill in the execution of rests in three-voice designs.

23 Right hand

24 Left hand

25 Right hand

At this point, or later at the discretion of the instructor, the collection *Manuals Only* (Augsburg Publishing House, 1965) may be introduced as supplementary material.

Chapter Four

Practice Habits

Learning proper practice habits and procedures is the most important single aspect of developing and mastering any musical skill or discipline. Improper practice usually does more harm than good, because it tends to strengthen and perpetuate mistakes and misconceptions. Ask yourself, as a student, what your aims and goals are in the practice room. What are you trying to achieve?

Here are some basic purposes of practice:
1. **Continuity.** The first skill to be developed is the ability to keep going, continuously, once you have begun to play. The organist must maintain the proper pace, without pause or hesitation, even if little things occasionally go wrong. Continuity is the backbone of organ playing, and the student must learn to "forge ahead," altering stops, correcting notes, thinking ahead, and adjusting balance as he plays. If the final desired tempo is too fast for present technical ability, by all means maintain a slower speed, but do keep it steady, sacrificing tempo for regularity. Much public performance is with others—accompanying choral groups and soloists, leading in hymn-singing, and playing with instrumental ensembles. Lagging and hesitancy cannot be permitted in such situations.
2. **Notes.** To develop accuracy
3. **Rhythm.** To develop precision and accuracy of rhythmic organization
4. **Tempo.** To develop steadiness and control of speed
5. **Organistic skills.** To develop control and coordination of manual and stop changes, the swell box, and other mechanical techniques of organ playing

In addition to the technical aspects outlined above, there are further artistic and aesthetic considerations as additional purposes of practice:
1. To memorize
2. To develop an awareness and mastery of style and interpretation
3. Occasionally, to sight-read
4. Occasionally, to practice transposition, modulation, improvisation, and related skills

It is rarely to your advantage to play through a piece only once and then proceed immediately to the next assigned piece. Play through a composition several times, with drill on difficult or troublesome passages, to build up concepts of style, accuracy, and control. At the same time, however, the student who is practicing continuity for a recital should occasionally play all his pieces through in sequence, without stopping to work on details.

Furthermore, if you make a mistake in note-playing, it is not wise merely to correct it and then proceed. Instead, every mistake constitutes a warning or sign that you have special work to do. Not only should you correct the mistake, but analyze it, altering any necessary fingering or pedaling. Next play the entire measure three or four times with note perfection, and then put it into context by playing it with the two or three previous and following measures several times, thus putting the passage together properly and working out the error.

Generally, if you make more than about one mistake per line (later, one or more mistakes per page), something is wrong; probably you are practicing too fast. Play so slowly that you can achieve note accuracy and at the same time maintain steadiness of tempo. Never slow down for the difficult passages and let it go at that. If you wish to increase the speed of a composition, then learn the harder sections so well that you can perform the entire work at a faster tempo.

Do not forget that accuracy of tempo and regularity of rhythm are basically fundamental to music, from the standpoint of projection to an audience. Therefore during much of your practice, maintain steadiness at all times even if it means occasionally sacrificing a note. But then, after you finish the composition, go back and, the next time through, work carefully and thoroughly for note accuracy. If you still cannot play with note accuracy, slow down yet more. If you are dissatisfied with your progress, check with the instructor for some other difficulty.

Sometimes you will have to spend an entire hour, or several hours, on one composition or on one small part of a piece. The musician who is striving for professional perfection must give long hours to the difficult task of practice. Learning to achieve in any subject involving mechanical skills requires hours and days and years of labor; sometimes there is a great deal of frustration and annoyance. The achievements are more than worth the anguish!

It is important to practice an hour or so as soon as you can after every lesson. This procedure provides a prompt check on corrections, criticisms, and suggestions. Otherwise you may forget and continue to practice errors in your pieces. Any time you find that you are becoming mentally fatigued, switch for a few minutes to another piece or page. Later you can return to the previous problem with renewed concentration.

When you are playing for your teacher at a lesson, always treat the situation as if it were a performance. That is, unless and until your instructor advises differently, when you make a mistake, do not stop for the purpose of correcting it, and then try to pick up the thread of musical continuity where you left off. Rather, attempt to keep going—leaving the error uncorrected for the time being—unruffled and not losing even a slight fraction of a beat. The teacher knows you slipped, and will stop you presently if he desires. If you were performing in public, a hymn or anthem accompaniment for example, you would never consider stopping to correct a note. The habit of continuity is most desirable to cultivate, especially when you are working on compositions from memory. This is not an attempt to "cover up" mistakes for the purpose of deceiving an audience. Rather, the reason for developing the ability to continue without pausing if a bit of difficulty is encountered, is a very real musical and artistic one. When you are projecting and portraying music, a slight note error, almost unnoticeable to the listener, does little damage to the presentation. However, any large break in the flow of continuous musical unfolding and development can almost shatter the musical experience for the listener: thus some of the effect of the piece is irrevocably lost. This is by no means an attempt to condone note mistakes or careless performing, but rather to restore emphasis to the musical values of the line, projected logically and continuously to the discerning audience (accuracy of notes has always been of vast importance to performer and listener alike).

The tape recorder is a useful device, and should not be overlooked as an adjunct to good practice. It is especially helpful in revealing rhythmic difficulties and artistic and stylistic inadequacies.

Here is a word of caution: when you are using a recorder to check on various musical and technical problems, it is often best not to play it back immediately: when you listen to your performance immediately thereafter, you do not really hear the machine because psychologically you are still "caught up" in your performance, and unless you are accustomed to working with recorders you merely hear what you thought you did, reconstructed and recreated. Rather, it is preferable to wait a day or two, or, better, a week, and then, when the immediate freshness of your performance has evaporated, play the tape. Thus you receive a more objective and impersonal evaluation of your playing (an interval of time, for the musical artist, is equivalent to distance—stepping back from the canvas—to the painter).

A tape recorder can be cruel to the performer, since it has an apparent tendency to exaggerate mistakes, tempo errors, and the like. Fortunately the casual listener, hearing an unfamiliar composition only once, is not tormented by the thoughts that run through the head of the performer as he listens to his own tapes!

Chapter Five

The Pedals: Heel and Toe

1 Left foot
Adagio, legato. mf, 4' or 2' only

It should be realized that at the point marked*, two separate and distinct mechanical operations take place: the toe releases; the heel attacks. These two events occur simultaneously. In order to separate these two operations for better analysis of the mechanical aspects of the problem, play the next exercise (No. 2) in which they do not occur simultaneously:

2 Left foot
Largo, legato. mp, 4' or 2' only

After executing and analyzing exercise 2, return to exercise 1 above. Alternate these two exercises until your ear tells you that you are achieving a smooth and precise legato in exercise 1.

3 Left foot
Same pitch and dynamic level as above.

4 Right foot

5 Right foot
Proceed with exercises 4 and 5 as with 1 and 2 above.

6 Right foot

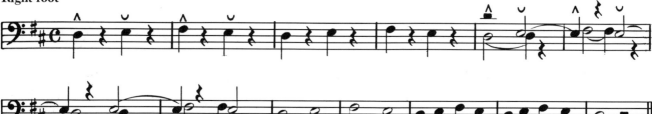

7 Left foot
Moderato, molto legato. mf, 16′, 8′, and 4′
Alternate toe and heel

8 Right foot
Moderato, molto legato. mf

It is occasionally necessary to change from heel to toe or from toe to heel of the same foot, on one note. (Pedaling indicated at exercises 9 through 12 is for drill purposes only, and would not normally be used for playing pedal scales).

9 Left foot
mf, 16′, 8′, and 4′

10 Left foot

11 Right foot

12 Right foot

13 Left foot
Adagio. mp, 8′ and 4′
Legato, heel and toe of the same foot

14 Right foot
Andante. mf, 8′, 4′, and 2′

15 Left foot
Quasi allegro. mf, 8′, 4′, and 2′
The student should work out his own pedaling, using heel and toe of the left foot only.

16 Right foot
Larghetto. mf, 8′ and 4′
Use heel and toe, maintaining careful legato.

The heel and toe of the same foot are sometimes required to span larger intervals, as in exercises 17 through 20.
17 Left foot drill
Adagio. f, 16′, 8′, and 4′

18 Left foot
Allegro molto

19 Right foot drill
Adagio

20 Right foot
Allegro molto

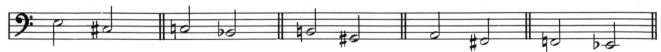

Recognize that the following major seconds and minor thirds "feel the same" to the foot, as far as stretch is concerned. The presence of the black key within the interval distinguishes the minor third:
21 Left foot

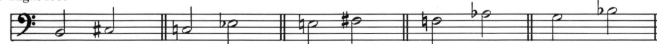

22 Right foot

37

The same foot may play two or more consecutive black keys by the correct use of the sole. Change from one side of the sole to the other by sliding quickly. No distinction in symbol (∧) is made for the left and right sides of the sole.

23 Left foot
Andantino. mp, 16', 8', and 4'

24 Right foot
Moderato. mp, 8' only

When no time signature appears, watch for unequal metres.
25 Heels and toes of both feet
Allegretto. p, 16' and 8'

Chapter Six

Phrasing

1 Right hand
Andante. mp, 8' and 4'
Observe the slurs, or phrase indications, in the following exercise.

2 Left hand

A method of execution of the phrase marking above is (1) release the final note of each phrase early (that is, hold the note slightly less than its indicated duration); (2) permit a brief moment of silence or "breath"; and (3) enter, in rhythm, or after an almost imperceptible delay, on the first beat of the next phrase. These steps happen quickly, and sound natural and logical to the listener.

The purpose of phrasing is to indicate the melodic structure of a composition so that the listener can best understand its "tune" or its thematic meaning and significance. Musical phrasing is intended to serve an aesthetic function similar to the literary or grammatical function of such punctuation marks as period, comma, or semicolon. There are, however, additional devices used by organists to indicate the shape and artistic structure of a musical line. Although the usual method, as described above, is lifting the final note of the phrase early, leaving a gap of silence in the line, and then attacking the first note of the succeeding phrase almost in tempo, there is another procedure which is often used. It seems to occur almost intuitively—controlled, it would appear, by the performer's subconscious mind. The significant notes within the phrase are dwelt on while slight ritards and accelerandos are inserted at phrase endings and beginnings. It takes much time and practice to achieve the subtleties of these rather difficult, and sometimes amorphous, artistic procedures; and more often than not the student finally masters them without being quite aware that he has done so. (The term "agogic accent" is often applied to the stress obtained by slightly lengthening the duration of a note.)

Observe proper phrasing in the following pedal exercises:

3 Both feet, heel and toe
Andante. mp, 16′, 8′, and 4′

4 Both feet, heel and toe
Andantino

Artistic growth takes place over a long period of time. Occasionally, the more a student practices deliberately to achieve artistic nuances, the more they seem to elude him. This is a common problem. At first the amateur organist, if he is sensitive, can detect that his phrasing attempts sound arbitrary and artificial. But time brings naturalness, control, and competence; with practice, convincing and logical-sounding phrasing will eventually become second-nature to the student. The goal is to control the medium completely, expressing, interpreting, and communicating with the authority of a professional musician.

At times the teacher will encourage students to try excesses of rubato in phrasing. This helps the less adventuresome student to "spread his wings"; he can be reined in later.

5 Left hand
Adagio. mp, 8′ and 4′
Additional drill in phrasing.

6 *Adagio. mp,* 16′, 8′, and 4′
The same theme as a study in pedal phrasing.

It should be noted that, in exercises 5 and 6, repeated note gaps and phrase breaks occur in conjunction with the same notes. As a rule, phrase breaks should have slightly longer intervals of silence than repeated note gaps. In other words, between the two B♭'s at A there is a longer moment of silence than between the two B♭'s at B. Similarly observe the F's at C and D. The specific problem of repeated notes will be examined in a later chapter.

Usually, all phrase breaks in a short composition are approximately the same.

Occasionally the comma symbol (,) is used instead of slur marks. At times the fermata (⌢) serves this function, but on other occasions it indicates its more usual meaning, hold or pause. In the absence of slurs or other phrase indications in a composition, the student may be permitted by the instructor to work out phrasings or breath marks at his own discretion, subject to the apparent and evident style of the piece. If the student has reservations about his artistic sense and musical background, and questions his own abilities to demonstrate a sensitivity toward phrasing, he may be assured that to some extent development of a mature concept of style is furthered by an imaginative experimental approach. If he makes serious phrasing mistakes, the instructor may explain why they are inappropriate, and draw him back to a more conservative approach. It is better to be bold and somewhat daring (if necessary, the instructor can point out misconceptions) than to be so cautious and over-prudent that one depends exclusively on the note-by-note guidance of the teacher. The imaginative student is already preparing himself for the time when he no longer has a teacher and must develop creative ideas of his own—and probably will himself instruct others.

Chapter Seven

Pedal Phrasing and Additional Aspects of Pedal Technique

Occasionally rests are written in, instead of phrasing indications. In such cases the performer should insert no additional phrase breaks. Legato is assumed between rests.

In the following pedal studies, use both feet, heel and toe as convenient.

1 *Adagio* (♩=50). *p*, Flute, 4', only

If there are metre changes, time signatures may be omitted at the discretion of the composer.

2 *Andante con moto* (♩=56). *mf*, 8', 4', and 2'

It is often necessary to substitute, or change feet on one note. This is one of the most important aspects of good pedal technique, because of its usefulness in sight-reading, improvising, and hymn playing. Substitution is considered more conducive to accuracy than crossing one foot over or under the other, where crossing involves wide skips. There are several ways of pedaling the following illustration. For purposes of this exercise, utilize substitution as indicated.

3 *Lento* (♩=c. 60). *p*, 16′, 8′, and 4′

4 *Allegretto. mf*, 16′, 8′, and 2′

5 *Largo ma non troppo* (𝅗𝅥=58). Flute 2', only, with tremulant

6 *Andantino* (♩=120). *mf*, 4' Principal only. Use heel, toe, and substitution, both feet.

7 *Moderato. pp*, Flute, 4', only. (Observe that cut-time moderato, having a 𝅗𝅥 unit of beat, is therefore faster than 4/4 moderato, with ♩ unit of beat).

It is sometimes necessary to substitute or change feet on a black key. This procedure, while quite possible, is more difficult than white key substitution.

8 *Moderato,* with quiet lyricism. *p,* 8′ and 4′

In detached and staccato pedal passages, care must be taken to execute the heel staccato notes with the same amount of spacing or detachment as those played by the toe.

9 *Adagio, non legato. pp,* Bourdon, 16′ and Gedeckt, 8′

10 *Quasi Presto. mp*, 8′ and 1′ or 8′ and 2′

Observe slurs and staccato notes in the next exercise.

11 *Adagio. mp*, 16′, 8′, and 4′

12 *Vivace, sempre staccato. f*, 16′, 8′, 4′, and 2′

Chapter Eight

Co-ordination

Two-voice coordination exercises are presented in this chapter. It is not necessary to practice the two lines separately unless difficulties are encountered.

Work out, and write in, fingering and pedaling in any troublesome passages.

Practice slowly at first; as technique and facility develop, increase to tempi as indicated.

1 *Allegretto* (♩=88)
Right hand. *mp*, 8′ and 4′

Pedal. *mp*, 16′, 8′, and 4′

2 *Allegro* (♩=63)
R. H. *mf*, 8′ and 2′

Ped. *mf*, 16′, 8′, and 4′

3 *Moderato* (♩ =104)
R. H. *mf*, 8′ solo stop, such as Krummhorn, Schalmei, or Oboe

Ped. *mp*, 16′, 8′, (and 4′ if desired)

4 *Largo* (♩ =58)
L. H. *mf*, 8′

Ped. *mp*, 16′ and 8′

5 *Andante con moto* (♩ =84)
L. H. *mp*, 8′ and 2′

Ped. *p*, 16′, 8′, and 4′

6 *Andante*
L. H. *mp*, 8 ′and 4′

Ped. *mp*, 16′, 8′, and 4′

7 *Allegro con brio*
R. H. *ff*, Principal chorus through mixture

Ped. *ff*, Principals, 16′ through mixture

8 *Moderato.* Release with precision at indicated rests.
R. H. *p*, 8′ or 8′ and 4′

Ped. *p*, 4′ only

9 *Adagio*
L. H. *mp,* solo stop, 4′ only

Ped. *p*, 4′ only

The student will encounter different metres in some contemporary compositions. Notice that time signatures for the two voices are different in exercise 10.

10 *Allegro*
L. H. *f*, 8′, 4′, and 2′

Ped. *f*, 16′, 8′, 4′, and 2′

In exercises 11 and 12, observe pitch instructions carefully. Pedal carries melody at higher pitch than the manual voice.

11 *Largo* (♪=104)
R. H. *p*, 8′ (and 16′ if available)

Ped. *mp*, 4′ solo stop *only*

Fine

D.C. al Fine

12 *Lento* (♩=58)
L. H. *p*, 8′ (and 16′, if available)

Ped. *mp*, 4′ solo stop *only*

13 *Allegro moderato* (♩=112)
L. H. *mf*, 8′ and 4′

Ped. *mf*, 16′, 8′, and 4′

53

14 *Vivace, quasi presto* (♪ =126)
R. H. *ff*, full, with mixtures and reeds

Ped. *ff* (without 32′ or heavier 16′ stops)

54

15 *Allegretto* (♩=108)
L. H. *mf*, 8′, 4′, and 2′

Ped. *mf*, 16′, 8′, 4′, and 2′

16 *Adagio*
L. H. *mp*, 8′, or 8′, 4′ solo

Ped. *p*, 16′ and 8′, or 16′, 8′, 4′

simile

non stacc.

poco rit.

a tempo

stacc.

rit.

non stacc.

As he plays a composition such as exercise 16, the student should be aware of certain artistic and aesthetic properties of the piece, and of some psychological phenomena which occur as the music unfolds.

The first consideration is melodic contours. Often, but not always, the melodic phrase progresses and evolves toward a high note, which usually occurs toward the end of the phrase, after which the melody tapers down to a cadence point. The student should recognize, for instance, that the first phrase of exercise 16 constitutes a 7½ measure melodic entity, which reaches its peak late in the phrase, at the high A in measure 6, after which it recedes, descending toward the A major tonal cadence. That high A is somewhat like a target, present in the background and waiting to be consummated, with the melody surging forward, struggling to reach it. The note is only attained after some "aesthetic wrestling"; once it is reached, the line fades away quickly. This particular melody features a number of ascending fragments. Notice that at the point of climax, the chord underlying the A is not tonic, but subdominant. The conflict between the note A and the non-tonic chord lends further tension, and a dynamic quality of unrest, forcing the line onward: it is aesthetically seeking, as it were, rest in the A major tonic tonality, which it finally achieves.

The student should react to these melodic contours, reaching onward with the melody, evolving and growing with it, and involving himself in it. This becomes an interaction which projects itself and communicates with the listener, thus clearly portraying the musical line for his understanding.

Another aspect of the aesthetic totality of a melody is its rhythmic context. Some melodies feature reiterated patterns, while variety is the keynote of others. Note the rhythmic patterns of the first 7½ measures:

Only two of the above patterns (line 1 and line 5) are identical. Here is a wide variety, deliberately conceived and constructed on the part of the composer. Since too much variety can lead to an incoherent whole, one looks for a unifying factor to counteract the multiplicity of rhythmic patterns, and it is found in the pedal, which uses completely consistent pizzicato quarters as a device to impart unity to the design.

The next qualities to be investigated are harmonic and polyphonic content. Since this design is a two-part structure, much of the harmony is implied, and is reconstructed in the listener's imagination. This reconstruction takes place quite actively, and, in this case, is given assistance by arpeggio figurations occuring in the melody (as in the first measure) which help spell out implied harmonies. The presence of two-part counterpoint in the design is quite clear. Contrary motion occurs often, and serves to control, to some extent, the wide range of the melody (which encompasses slightly more than two octaves, from C# to d²).

57

Some other structural elements which the student should analyze are:
1. modulation and the locations of any extended sequences featuring chromatics
2. the formal construction of the composition
   (This is a short three-part "da capo" design, ABA, with some thematic allusions to A recurring in B, and the return of A preceded by a preparatory dominant pedal point.)
3. metre
   (The straight undeviating $\frac{4}{4}$ metre lends stability and gravity to this piece.)
4. tempo
   (The combination of variety of rhythms within the melody, the lyrical quality of the composition, and the construction of the pedal line dictate a slow tempo for the piece.)

The student need not spend too much time analyzing the musical content and structure of exercises in an instruction book, but ought to become increasingly aware of the facets of music, so that later when he is performing compositions from the established organ concert repertoire he may spend considerable time in profitable artistic analysis.

17 *Allegro molto con brio*
R. H. *ff*, 8', 4', 2' and mixture

59

Chapter Nine

Trios

In three-staff organ trio writing, the right hand is always assigned the upper staff, left hand the middle staff, and pedal the lower. However, the right hand is not necessarily assigned to the upper manual: either hand can perform on either manual, depending on stops and timbres desired. It is wise to alternate manuals frequently.

Registration: for the manuals, select two independent contrasting combinations, each built on basic 8′ pitch, and of about the same volume. For the pedal, stops of at least 16′ and 8′ pitch should be represented, unless otherwise noted.

1 *Moderato. mp*

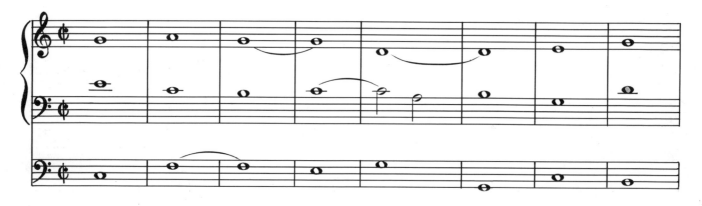

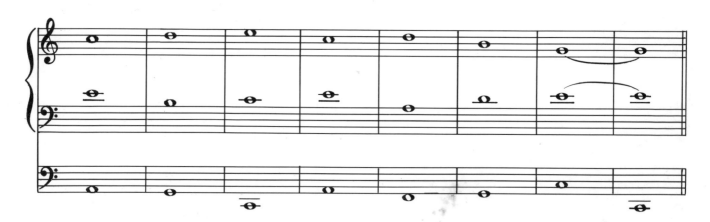

2 *Allegretto. mf*

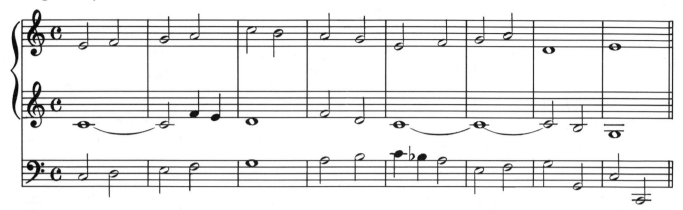

3 *Adagio. p*

4 *Andantino. mf*

61

5 *Andante.* Some voice-crossing occurs.

6 *Adagio. p*

7 *Largo. p* This may be played with both hands on the same manual.

63

8 *Moderato. mp*

poco rit.

64

9 *Allegretto. mf*

Fine

D.C. al Fine

65

10 *Allegro molto.* Full organ

11 *Larghetto.* Pedal melody. Observe pitch instructions carefully, avoiding stops of 16′ or 8′ pitch in pedal.

12 *Moderato. p* Contemporary chord structure

13 Theme and two variations. *Note:* When a new time-signature appears above the staff, it signifies a temporary change for the one measure only, immediately followed by a return to the basic metre. In every such case, ♪ = ♪ unless specified otherwise by the composer.

Both hands on Great, 8′, 4′, and 2′. *mf*
Allegretto

69

R.H. *Legato*
Gt. Trumpet 8′ *ff*

L.H. *Staccato*
Sw. 8′, 4′, and 2′, *f*

Ped. 16′, 8′, 4′, *f*

non staccato

Both hands on Gt.

Full chorus with reeds, *ff*

L. H. plays alto in either clef

Ped.

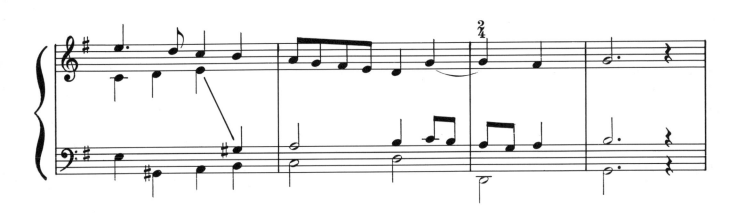

14 A Toccata
Both hands on Great. In free, flexible rhythm.

In steady, strict rhythm, fast

75

Chapter Ten

Alternate Toes

It is occasionally necessary for one foot to cross over or under the other. Either foot may be forward, depending on convenience and ease of execution of the passage.

The student should keep the toe of whichever foot is forward close to the black keys at all times; otherwise he may, without realizing it, gradually permit the forward foot to slide or crawl backward, thus crowding and hampering the other foot until it cannot function properly.

Vivace:

The presence of black keys in a passage naturally determines which foot must be forward, since it is virtually impossible for the heel to play black keys.

For the sake of precision and clear, clean articulation, alternate toes are preferable to heel-and-toe usage in passages like the following:

is better than:

However, notice proper use of the heel in the following passage:

And in the following: also good:

Allegretto

Chapter Eleven

Repeated Notes

One of the difficult artistic problems in organ playing centers in the execution of repeated notes. The fact that there are a number of different theories and approaches points up the extent of the problem.

The difficulty stems from a basic element of organ construction. One of the mechanical features of the organ as an instrument is the fact that, once the key is depressed and a tone initiated, the sound remains at the same dynamic level indefinitely, and does not die away; it continues at full volume until the key is released. Furthermore, if the same note follows immediately, it is not possible to release and attack the same key at the same time. It follows that the key must be released a little prematurely in order that it be struck again at the proper moment. This leaves a gap of silence. The problem is, how long should that interval be?

1 For example, the following passage

2 could be performed as follows:

3 or as follows:

or with rests somewhere between ▬ and ↯ .

The decision regarding the amount of rest inserted between repeated notes depends on several factors: (1) tempo of performance; (2) size of room and amount of reverberation; (3) registration and volume; (4) pitch, whether high or low; and (5) voice (soprano, bass or inner voice; melody or accompaniment).

The pattern of notes given in exercise 1 is found in all the illustrations below. The student should experiment with large and small gaps (each example may require that the repeated notes lose a different proportion of their value), deciding for himself the best procedure in each case. The instructor may play these examples for the student, if desired.

80

8 *Moderato*

mp, 8', 4', and 2'

With Pedal, 16', coupled

etc.

9 *Andante*

ff Full Organ

ff Full Pedal

etc.

In general, it may be said that longer intervals are required in buildings with long reverberation periods. Fast music requires that repeated notes lose proportionately more of their value than slow music; intricate, contrapuntal and/or intensely dissonant music demands breaks if repeated notes are to be heard; and repeated notes at moderate tempi, in voices where they can be heard distinctly, do not require such large breaks. The number of people in a room may also be a determining factor. In conclusion it may be said that the exact spacings of repeated notes cannot be determined once and for all, but must be decided individually in the light of the circumstances under which they occur.

Chapter Twelve

The Manuals: Repeated Notes and Voice Leading

Execute manual repeated notes clearly with large, ample breaks between notes. For these exercises, try to make all gaps the same length. The fingers should move with clean articulation.

1 Right hand *Adagio. p, 8′ only*

In exercise 1, the student should decide how long the spaces ought to be, at *, for best artistic effect.

2 Left hand
Allegretto. mp, 8′ and 2′

In the following exercises, maintain meticulous legato in each voice except where repeated notes occur; think of each voice as an independent melodic line. Use finger substitutions when necessary. Write in fingering if you wish.

3 Right hand
Andantino. mf, 8′ Flute and 4′ Principal

4 Right hand

5 Left hand

6 Left hand

7 A special problem is presented by a situation in which one voice enters a unison with another voice, as follows:

8 The voice moving into the unison takes precedence over the stationary voice, forcing it to break and repeat. Exercise 7 is performed as follows:

Observe that the break in the alto voice, in exercise 8, may be more or less than an eighth rest, depending upon speed and other factors.

9 If the alto note is tied through, rather than broken in preparation for the soprano, the passage sounds as if it were written as follows:

The above interpretation is usually avoided as it seems to defeat the melodic intent of the composer.

10 Observe, therefore, that the two following passages, which are written differently, sound alike:

11 *Note:* avoid inserting a break between the third and fourth soprano notes, G and D.

On the other hand, notice the difference between the two following examples:

12

13

14 Exercise 12 is played as follows:

15 But exercise 13 is played:

In other words, in exercises 12 and 14, the continuous flow of the alto whole notes is sacrificed for the soprano melody, while in exercises 13 and 15 the legato of the soprano melody is sacrificed for the repeated notes of the alto voice.

16 A somewhat similar situation is found in the case of repeated notes between two voices:

17 When clean articulation or rhythmic impulse is the important consideration, the passage should be played in the following manner:

18 The spacings inserted in the above exercise are for the purpose of avoiding the following aural illusion:

19 Some authorities state that when the soprano ascends in a repeated note situation,

it can be heard distinctly, and therefore the repeated notes should be tied.

However, when the soprano descends,

they advocate breaking the repeated notes and inserting a distinct gap for the sake of clarity.

A very few authorities, on the other hand, tie through all such repeated notes, both ascending and descending. In the last analysis, the ear of the player must be the judge. The notes may be tied, or released and repeated. Which sounds best? If clarity is most important, especially when one of the voices is the soprano, it is desirable to break and repeat the duplicated note. On the other hand, when smoothness and maximum legato are primary considerations, especially in inner voices, the note ought to be tied. (The professional performer has available under his control varying sizes, or durations, of breaks and rests which he utilizes in different musical situations).

20 Left hand
mp, 8', 4' and 2'. Practice the following drill slowly at first. Gradually increase tempo to *allegro*.

21 Right hand

22 Both hands

Lento (♩ =56). *p*. Flutes and voix celestes. When phrase indications appear as below, identical for soprano and bass, any and all inner voices follow the same phrasing, unless a different procedure is indicated in the score.

23 Repeated notes, three voices

Largo (♩=76). Practice left hand alone first, using finger substitutions as necessary.

R. H. *mp*, Flutes, 8′ and 4′ or solo stop 8′

L. H. *p*, 8′

poco rit.

Slightly faster

Tempo I

poco rit . . . .

ritard. _ _ _ _ _ _ _ _

24 *Allegro*
Energetic and forceful.

f (Second time *ff*)

A word of caution: the effect of dotted rhythms is vitiated if they are allowed to deteriorate into triplet patterns. In exercise 12 above, continually guard against permitting the 𝄽 pattern to drift into 𝄽. The usual way of preventing this error is by counting eighths.

Occasionally in a four-part design for manuals alone, the interval between bass and tenor becomes so large that temporarily the right hand must take the tenor, even though it is not indicated in the music. When this occurs, legato and independence of voice leading must be carefully maintained.

25 *Andante*
mp, Principal 8′

26 Transfer of alto voice between hands
(Be sure to release note when other hand picks up the alto voice.) It is inadvisable to transfer the alto line between two different sounds. Therefore, when a musical situation is encountered in which there are three or more manual voices and it is mechanically necessary for one voice to switch between hands, one manual is artistically better than two—otherwise the transferring voice changes tone color arbitrarily rather than for aesthetic reasons.

Very slowly
String and/or flute celestes 8′ and 4′, *p*.

Allegretto

Gt. 8' and 2' *mp*

(L.H.)

92

27 Tenor transfers between hands

(Watch voice leading: at no time, except in last measure, should five notes be played at any one time.)

Chapter Thirteen

Three Special Problems in Voice Leading

1 Leaving a unison

When two voices leave a unison at different times, as in the above example (the dot refers only to the alto note), care must be taken not to substitute a rest for the dot.

Avoid: Also incorrect:

2 A dissonant cadence

In the above example, do not release the alto F♯ when the soprano descends to the eighth note G. This temporary acute dissonance (which is characteristic of the Baroque Period) accentuates the concord of the unison which follows: this desirable contrast is preserved by proper execution of the passage.

3 Crossing of voices

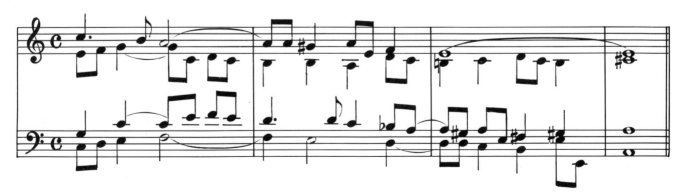

Play the voices which cross with either hand—whichever is easiest and most convenient. That is, it is not necessary to play such excerpts "as written." Composers write passages thus for a variety of reasons: to give interest or prominence to a tenor line, for example, or to avoid prohibited progressions (as parallel fifths in this illustration).

Sometimes voices cross within one hand. This is indicated by reversed stems, as follows:

If there are any doubts or ambiguities about such a passage, it should be first separated into its components:

Soprano: Alto:

Chapter Fourteen

Co-ordination: Repeated Notes

1 Moderate

Care must be taken in exercise 1 to execute the $\frac{3}{4}$ 𝅘𝅥𝅭 𝅘𝅥𝅮 𝅘𝅥 precisely and accurately.

Unless the player is on his guard, this pattern often deteriorates into $\frac{9}{8}$ 𝅘𝅥𝅭 𝅘𝅥 𝅘𝅥𝅮𝅘𝅥

or $\frac{3}{4}$ 𝅘𝅥 𝅘𝅥𝅭𝅘𝅥𝅮 𝅘𝅥 Keep check by counting $\frac{3}{4}$ 𝅘𝅥𝅭 𝅘𝅥𝅮 𝅘𝅥

1 and 2 and 3 and.

2 A different triple metric organization
Slowly

3 Four parts, with repeated notes
Adagio. mp, Swell, Flutes and Strings, 8′, and Flute, 4′

Ped. *mp* 16′, 8′ (and 4′)

98

99

4 Repeated notes in left hand

Moderate

Practice this exercise as follows:

(1) L.H. alone   (4) R. H. and L. H.
(2) L. H. and Ped.   (5) All voices
(3) R. H. alone

R. H. *p*, 8′ and 2′, or 8′ and 1′; R. H. sempre staccato

L. H. *mp*, 8′ and 4′; L. H. melody, legato

Ped. *p*, 16′ and 8′

R. H. non
staccato

100

5 *Andante*

Watch metre change (♩ = ♩ throughout)

pp 8′ and 4′

pp 16′ and 8′

ritard . . . .

6 Pedal melody

Moderately fast

Use one of the following combinations:
R. H. 4′ only; L. H. 4′ only; Ped. 2′ only; or
R. H. 8′ only; L. H. 8′ only; Ped. 4′ only.

7 A problem in reading $\frac{4}{2}$ time, with ♩ unit of beat

Not too slowly

Note: the 𝄎, or double whole note, is called the "breve."

The collection *MUSIC FOR WORSHIP with Easy Pedals* (Augsburg Publishing House, 1966) may be used as supplementary material.

Chapter Fifteen

The Hymn

One of the organist's most important duties is hymn playing. The hymn represents an opportunity for congregational participation in corporate worship, and should be considered important in the organist's allotment of preparation time. Hymns must be practiced carefully and played competently.

The hymn as such is a composition written basically for choir. As a musical instrument, the choir is different from the organ in style, techniques and abilities. Therefore when organists play hymns they essentially transcribe—that is, they play compositions which were primarily intended for another type of instrument. Some adjustments are necessarily required.

From the mechanical standpoint, the right hand normally plays soprano and alto parts, the left hand plays the tenor line, and the bass notes are played on the pedals. Although later the left hand may be permitted to double the pedals and play the bass notes also (the performer's ear deciding on the merits of this doubling), it is best at first for the beginner to play only the tenor with the left hand, forcing an independent approach to the pedals.

Repeated notes are a fundamental problem. The human voice has relatively little trouble with repeated notes, but the organ—especially the pedals—has difficulty making a large number of repeated notes sound musical. They are contrary to the innate and inherent characteristics of the instrument. Therefore the following principle is observed: do not necessarily play all the notes as written on the page, but tie through certain repeated notes. In general, all soprano notes are repeated; alto and tenor voices may be tied or repeated at the discretion of the organist, depending on the hymn, the tempo, and possible occasional sluggishness of the congregation in singing. Repeated pedal notes may be broken or tied, depending on circumstances. A safe procedure in the average moderate-sized sanctuary is to tie repeated pedal notes. Repeated pedal notes sound especially awkward on some electronic instruments. In larger buildings, however, especially when dealing with brisk, energetic hymns, repeated pedal notes may be detached somewhat; in softer, slower meditative hymns all such notes may be tied. If the congregation tends to drag, it may be necessary to detach all pedal notes quite crisply for a few measures, so that the congregation may be "pulled along." In general, pedal repeated notes are not tied over a barline ("Joy to the world" would be an exception to this principle).

Other than the above-mentioned considerations in regard to repeated notes, legato is the normal procedure in hymn playing. At phrase endings, some organists break all voices for a short gap of silence, while others break all voices except the pedal, carrying it through legato or tied to the beginning of the next phrase. The procedure of maintaining the bass note and keeping it sounding through phrase breaks has some adherents because it avoids leaving the congregation, especially the men, feeling "stranded" and awkward at phrase endings. However, there is some merit in the crisp, clean effect of leaving a gap in all voices at phrase endings, especially since it tends to impart rhythmic vigor to the next entrance.

Some organists play the bass line one octave lower than written. This practice usually ought to be avoided; it depends to some extent on the nature of the hymn being played, and also on whether or not the organ has a weak pedal division. When first learning hymns, students should play pedal notes as written.

A hymn consists of two elements: words and music. Organists must not lose sight of the fact that the music is a vehicle for the words, which are important. In order not to distort the meaning of the text, it is advisable for the organist to observe the more important punctuation marks. This means that sometimes a slight break occurs in the middle of a musical phrase (but this must not be overexaggerated); and sometimes the end of a musical phrase must be carried over without a break, legato, into the beginning of the next phrase (but without hurrying or otherwise distorting the rhythm). Obviously when a great many commas occur in sequence in the text, there is no need to observe all of them.

The organ student should have his own hymnal, and write in, if he desires, pedaling and fingering for difficult or treacherous passages. In preparation for the Sunday service, hymns should be practiced diligently, with some time devoted to a study of the words of each stanza. An unexpected repeat or *Da Capo* should be marked! The organist should make a note of registration changes required by certain stanzas.

Organists should, however, often practice unfamiliar hymns without working out pedaling beforehand, or writing it in, but rather *thinking* it ahead; this is for the purpose of improvement in sight-reading. All professional organists can recall occasions upon which a hymn number was suddenly and spontaneously changed, and they were forced to sight-read immediately in public; so this skill must be learned competently by every potential church organist.

Tempo, registration, volume, and general style and interpretation depend on the words of the hymn, the season, the congregation's singing abilities and habits, and so forth, and will be found to vary quite a bit. Sometimes it is appropriate to vary the registration with the stanzas of a hymn, or reharmonize the last stanza, or improvise a descant upon one or more stanzas. Avoid doing anything just for the sake of showing off, but do not hesitate to do something spectacular if there are legitimate spiritual and artistic reasons for so doing. Suitable, proper, and inspiring hymn-playing can assist materially in fostering attitudes of worship. The organ, handled majestically, can seem almost to speak with the voice of the authority of the Holy Spirit; on the other hand it sometimes serves as the voice of a contrite congregation, speaking with humility.

Occasionally practice transposing hymns, one-half step up and down and a whole step up and down.

Sometimes practice "soloing out" the soprano alone with the right hand on a separate manual, with a prominent solo stop; in such a case the left hand takes the alto and tenor voices, and pedal "takes" the bass. This procedure is useful when announcing an unfamiliar hymn, as the contours of the melody are then clearly defined.

In situations where the "Amens" are sung, they generally ought to be played as loud as the body of the hymn. Do not apologize for an "Amen" by suddenly quieting down for it. "Amen," meaning, "so be it," is an affirmation of the meaning of the text just sung—a promise to abide by it and to live in accordance with its teachings.

Added notes are permissable only under certain conditions. It is legitimate to add the fifth to the last chord of a hymn in which, for reasons of voice-leading, only the third is present, if this procedure gives depth to the chord, for better support of congregational singing. It is not appropriate to add sevenths to dominant chords, or for the most part to any other chords (except during a freely harmonized stanza).

Count the full three or four beats at phrase endings. The congregation will learn to depend on this procedure, coming in with a vigorous entrance at the beginning of the next phrase, confident that the organ will be there.

In order that the symbols found in hymnals be made clear, a sample page is reproduced below, with some explanatory comments:

Holy Communion

DUNDEE (French). C. M.
In moderate time, with dignity

Scottish Psalter, 1615

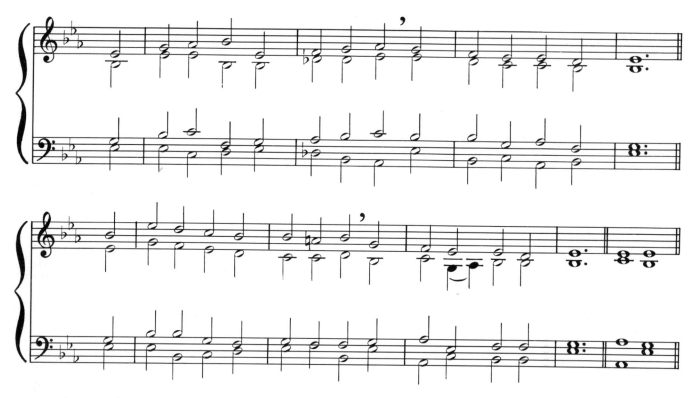

1. According to thy gracious word,
   In meek humility,
   This will I do, my dying Lord,
   I will remember thee.

2. And when these failing lips grow dumb,
   And mind and memory flee,
   When thou shalt in thy kingdom come,
   Jesus, remember me. Amen.

James Montgomery, 1771-1854

This hymn may also be sung to LONDON NEW (No. 381)

The two components of the above hymn are words and music, or poem and tune. The name of the tune is *Dundee*, although in some hymnals it is given the name French. We are not told who wrote the tune, but it first appeared in *Scottish Psalter* in 1615. The name of the poem is "According to Thy Gracious Word." If not otherwise indicated, it is common practice to assign a religious poem its first line as title. The words were written by James Montgomery, 1771-1854. The metric organization of the tune is C. M., or Common Metre; that is, 8 6 8 6, which signifies a tune of four lines, alternating eight and six syllables. The metric organization of the poem is obviously also C. M.; otherwise they could not be used together. This hymn would normally be used at a service of Holy Communion. The editors of this hymnal offer an alternative tune, *London New*, No. 381 in this particular hymnal, if this musical setting is unfamiliar. Performance instructions are given: "In moderate time, with dignity." The metre is 4/2, but the time signature is omitted. Modern hymnals are getting away from metre indications for two reasons: end-of-phrase fermati are often written out, thus changing the metre more frequently; and performers are now being encouraged to interpret hymns more freely and with slightly more flow, rather than square rigidity.

The following hymns are provided for practice. Each presents a somewhat different artistic or technical problem. Words are given in each case. In playing these hymns, the words should be interpreted in a general way, rather than too literally, word for word; practice changing registration for each stanza if the words seem to require it.

(For further information on hymn performance, see *A Guide to Effective Hymn Playing* by Margaret Sihler Anderson, Augsburg Publishing House, 1964)

I. Radnor

Metre: L. M. ("Long Metre," 8 8. 8 8.)

Version A

1. We ask no greater joy, O Lord,
   Than to respond when thou dost call,
   And talents given by thee employ
   To make thy realm encompass all.

2. We know not whither thou wilt guide,
   Nor yet the part that we must play;
   By faith we trust thy constant grace
   And stedfast tread thy holy way.

3. Then let us with good courage toil,
   Though others' gifts our own exceed;
   When earnestly we work for thee,
   We pray, O Father, bless the deed.

4. Give strength, O Lord, to heart and hand;
   Bold faith and courage grant, we pray;
   Incline our minds to seek thy will,
   Our hearts to love thee and obey.

Barbara J. Owen

Version B

Execution, following the words as at stanza 1 (♩ =c. 116).

This hymntune presents the problem of repeated soprano notes. For clarification, two versions are given above, A as it would appear in a hymnal, and B a probable execution in the average small sanctuary. Bear in mind, however, that performance of repeated notes varies, depending on acoustics and many other factors. Note that the alto break in first measure (B) helps to establish tempo clearly; such articulation gives animation and occasional rhythmic vitality.

II. DeWitt

Metre: C. M. ("Common Metre," 8 6. 8 6.)

Moderately Slow

1. O God of love, who gavest life,
   What shall we give to thee,
   Whose wealth is all the universe,
   Whose time eternity?

2. Take thou, O Lord, our humble hearts,
   Devoted to thy praise,
   Our very selves—in gratitude
   To serve thee all our days.

3. Thus we would give our precious time,
   Each dedicated hour,
   To be an offering blest of thee
   To make thy church a power.

4. And all the talents that we have
   We pray thee use, O Lord,
   To magnify thy glorious Name
   And spread abroad thy word.

5. So then with heart and time and skills
   All given in love to thee,
   We gladly share our earthly goods
   To bless humanity.

E. Urner Goodman

Words from *Ten New Stewardship Hymns,* copyright 1961 by the Hymn Society of America. Used by permission. This tune may also be used with "There is a green hill far away," and "Alas, and did my Saviour bleed."

This hymntune presents the problem of entire chords repeated.

*Suggested methods of execution of the measure indicated:

III. Nancy

Metre: 9 8. 9 8. 8 8.

Briskly

1. Give to the Lord, as he has blessed thee.
   Even when he seems far away,
   Know that his love has e'er possessed thee,
   Shelters and feeds thee every day.
   Heaven and earth are God's alone:
   Wilt thou hold back from him his own?

2. Give to the Lord, as he has blessed thee,
   Kept thee and guided from thy birth;
   Look to the day when death will wrest thee
   From all thy treasures here on earth.
   God hath rich gifts for thee above;
   Give of thy substance, now, in love.

3. Give to the Lord, as he has blessed thee,
   Who pours forth bounties rich and full;
   Let all thy selfish aims confessed be;
   Gain not the world, and lose thy soul!
   Put all thou hast in God's own hands,
   In trust obeying his commands.

James Boeringer

IV. David's Tune

Metre: C. M.

1. May church and Christian home combine
   To teach thy perfect way,
   With gentleness and love like thine,
   That none shall ever stray.

2. Let all unworthy aims depart,
   Imbue us with thy grace,
   Within the home let every heart
   Become thy dwelling-place.

3. Shine, Light Divine; reveal thy face
   Where darkness else might be.
   Grant, Love Divine, in every place
   Glad fellowship with thee.

4. May stedfast faith and earnest prayer
   Keep sacred vows secure;
   Build thou a hallowed dwelling where
   True joy and peace endure.

Carlton C. Buck

Words from *Thirteen New Marriage and Family Life Hymns,* copyright 1961 by the Hymn Society of America. Used by permission. This tune may also be used with "Now that the day-star glimmers bright," "Behold us, Lord, a little space," "Father of mercies, in Thy word," and "O God, accept my heart this day."

This tune is a contemporary setting. Keep quarter notes constant at metre changes. On one or more stanzas, tenor line may be used as descant or as countermelody—solo stop on separate manual.

V. Three-Tone Melody

Metre: C. M.

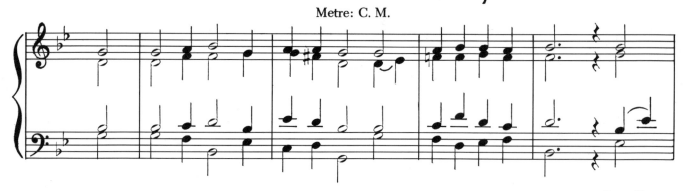

Last Stanza:

1. O Master Teacher, teach us now
   That we in turn may teach;
   Reveal thy truth and teach us how
   The hearts of men to reach.

2. Enlighten now each seeking mind
   With thy great mind of love;
   That in our seeking we may find
   The wisdom from above.

3. Instruct our souls that we may learn
   The lessons of the heart;
   That taught by thee, we may in turn
   Thy saving truth impart.

4. Give us a grasp upon thy word,
   The truth that comes from thee;
   Help men to teach till all have heard,
   And every mind is free.

Carlton C. Buck

Words from *Fifteen New Christian Education Hymns,* copyright 1959 by the Hymn Society of America. Used by permission. This tune may also be used with: "The Lord will come and not be slow," and "Lord, in thy Name thy servants plead."

In this tune, although the measures seem to have metres of $\frac{6}{4}$, $\frac{3}{2}$ and $\frac{4}{4}$, think of the $\frac{6}{4}$ as syncopated $\frac{3}{2}$ and the $\frac{4}{4}$ as $\frac{2}{2}$; the unit of beat thus becomes a half-note. Do not play this tune too fast (M. M. $\quad$ =c. 60).

An alternate version of this tune is given below:

Last Stanza:

VI. God of the Ages

Metre: L. M.

Broadly; with great dignity

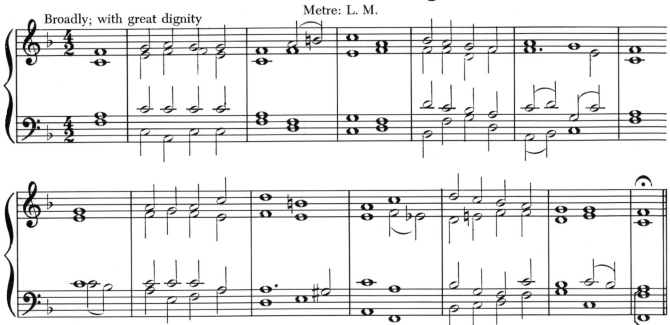

1. God of the ages, by whose hand
   Through years long past our lives were led,
   Give us new courage now to stand,
   New faith to find the paths ahead.
2. Thou art the Thought beyond all thought,
   The Gift beyond our utmost prayer;
   No farthest reach where thou art not,
   No height but we may find thee there.

3. Forgive our wavering trust in thee,
   Our wild alarms, our trembling fears;
   In thy strong hand eternally
   Rests the unfolding of the years.
4. Though there be dark, uncharted space,
   With worlds on worlds beyond our sight,
   Still may we trust thy love and grace,
   And wait thy word, let there be light.

Elisabeth Burrowes

Words from *Twelve New World Order Hymns*, copyright 1958 by the Hymn Society of America. Used by permission. This tune may also be used with "O Trinity of blessed light," "New every morning is the love," and "Awake, my soul, and with the sun."

This tune may also be used with: Praise God, from whom all blessings flow;
                                      Praise him, all creatures here below;
                                      Praise him above, ye heavenly host;
                                      Praise Father, Son, and Holy Ghost.   Thomas Ken, 1637-1711.

Following is an alternate harmonization of the same tune, to be sung in unison:

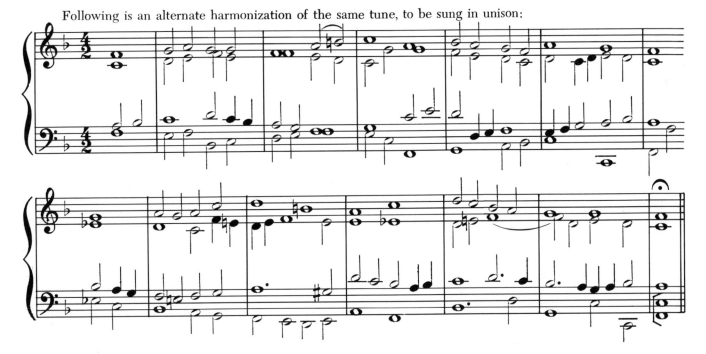

VII. Kendall

Metre: 8 7. 8 7. D. (D=doubled)

1. God of all, who art our Father,
   In our homes thyself make known
   Through thy Holy Spirit's fervor,
   Through the grace which thou hast shown;
   When life's tensions crowd upon us,
   Fill our homes with wisdom true;
   Through the Savior's living presence
   Manifest thyself anew.

2. Should the gift of sons and daughters,
   Light our homes and bring us joy;
   Grant to them thy strength and wisdom,
   Faith that nothing can destroy.
   Hear them when their hearts are contrite,
   Guidance give throughout their days;
   Furnish each with growing insight
   And reveal to them thy ways.

3. Unto thee, who art our Father,
   Come we, all mankind, in praise;
   Each to each is thus a brother,
   As we join to seek thy ways.
   Let no man neglect another
   Heedless of his brother's call;
   Let thy love unite us ever
   Binding close thy children all.

Walter N. Vernon

VIII. Hoiness

Metre: C. M. D.

1. O God, thy hand the heavens made
   And all that they contain;
   The world appeared at thy command,
   And in it thou shalt reign.
   The restless sea, the land, the sky,
   Thy handiwork declare;
   The touch of thy creative pow'r
   Is present everywhere.

2. To men are given gifts divine,
   All talents thou dost send;
   Inspire us now to use them well,
   Thy kingdom to extend.
   We hold each gift a trust from thee,
   Nor claim it as our own;
   We gratefully acknowledge, Lord,
   All things are thine alone.

3. Deliver us from selfish aims,
   True stewards we would be;
   Endow us with a deep desire
   To share with men and thee.
   A full accounting we must give,
   The Master we shall face;
   Let us approach his throne with joy
   Supported by thy grace.

Frank Leroy Cross

IX. Donald Hugh

Metre: L. M.

Stanza 1

Stanza 2

Alternate harmonization for Stanza 3 (Unison)

Without Ped. L.H. Combination similar to R.H. but include 16′.

Stanza 4. Melody in Alto (Unison)

With Ped.

1. O Master Teacher of mankind,
   Incarnate love in thee we find;
   In thee we see the Father's face;
   In thee we find his heavenly grace.

2. May we accept courageously
   The great commission giv'n by thee:
   "Go teach the message that I give,
   That all may see, and all may live."

3. O Teacher of the truth divine,
   We would be followers of thine,
   And dedicate our lives to thee,
   To teach thy truth and set men free.

4. Create within us all, thy mind;
   Teach us to seek that we may find;
   Teach us to love that we may lift
   Before all men God's heav'nly Gift.

Words from *Fifteen New Christian Education Hymns*, copyright 1959 by the Hymn Society of America. Used by permission.

X. Teal

Metre: 8 7. 8 7. 8 8 7.

120

1. O Lord our God, from far and near
   We come to raise our voices,
   To sing thy praise, O Savior dear,
   In whom our heart rejoices;
   Thy presence, Lord, we seek each day;
   Be thou our guide, our help, and stay;
   Hear us, O Lord, we pray thee.

2. Thy people, Lord, have gathered here
   To ask of thee thy blessing;
   Thy mercy, Lord, is ever near,
   We come our sins confessing;
   Where we have failed to show our light,
   Where we have failed to love aright,
   Forgive, O Lord, we pray thee.

3. To us, O Lord, is thy command
   To tell salvation's story
   To erring souls in every land
   Make known the King of Glory;
   Souls still in bondage, lost in sin,
   Grant us thy grace their hearts to win
   For thee, O Lord, we pray thee.

4. The work is thine, O Christ our Lord,
   The work here now before us;
   The foe is strong, yet in thy word
   Thy promises restore us;
   The gates of hell cannot prevail,
   Our fathers' God, he cannot fail,
   All praise to thee for ever.

Elizabeth K. Wedel

Words used by permission, Faith and Life Press, Newton, Kansas.
Words from *Centennial Hymns,* copyright 1959, and written for the centennial of the General Conference, Mennonite Church.
This tune may also be used with "Let all the multitudes of light" and "Sing praise to God who reigns above."

This contemporary setting is designed to be sung in unison. Note time changes, as indicated. When first introducing a new hymntune with unfamiliar or somewhat unusual harmonizations, it is well to play the first stanza or two in unison (actually, octaves) only. Otherwise the soprano note, as at * and **, for example, may tend to be obscured and learned incorrectly because of the initially disconcerting harmony.

XI. St. Olaf College

Metre: C. M.

With vigor

1. As did the Christ, we'll undertake
   God's workmen bold to be,
   For he whose skill is in our hands
   Depends on you and me.

2. O Christ, we rise with eager joy
   To follow in thy way;
   We offer heart and mind and soul
   To do thy work today.

3. As teacher, farmer, housewife, clerk
   Whate'er the call may be,
   Each one at his appointed task
   In service honors thee.

Dorothy Fay Ross

Words from *Three More New Hymns for Youth by Youth,* copyright 1957 by the Hymn Society of America. Used by permission. This tune may also be used with "Put forth, O God, thy Spirit's might," and "O for a thousand tongues to sing."

Play this tune with energy and animation. Note that the half-note is the unit of beat in cut time ($\mathcal{C}$ or $\frac{2}{2}$); treat it as one would treat a quarter-note in $\frac{2}{4}$ time. Thus quarter notes in this example become the equivalent of eighth notes. Practice transposing this hymntune to the key of G.

XII. The Western Sky

Metre: L. M.

Slowly and meditatively

1. O may thy Church build bridges, Lord,
   Across the wastes where men have warred,
   With stone on stone as fightings cease
   And warfare yields to lasting peace.

2. Forgiveness, justice, in each span
   As man is reconciled to man,
   And enmity and hate and fear
   Give way to love and hope and cheer.

3. Lord, let these bridges ever be
   For rich and poor, from sea to sea,
   Across which man may still progress
   And not destroy the world, but bless.

4. O teach us thus to build for peace,
   And may our efforts never cease
   Till nations press with one accord
   Into the kingdom of our Lord!

Elizabeth Patton Moss

XIII. Cassler

Metre: L. M.

1. From hearts around the world, O Lord,
   Through centuries of blind discord,
   There is one prayer which does not cease;
   The people yearn and grope for peace.

2. Though war and hate have been man's lot,
   The dream, the hope, of peace die not.
   Let nothing move our hearts from thee,
   Apart from whom no peace can be.

3. Lord, use thy Church to point the way;
   May we thy clear commands obey;
   Be reconciled, forgive and bless;
   May peace proceed from righteousness.

4. Lord, we confess our greed and pride,
   The scorn of men for whom Christ died,
   The prejudice, neglect, and hate,
   The love of wealth and power too great.

5. Grant us our Master's heart and mind,
   His care for all the poor and blind,
   For every race, for young and old,
   Despised, rejected, hungry, cold.

6. Let us not lose the vision blest,
   The dream of peace, the hope, the quest;
   Thy gracious will be done each day;
   Thy kingdom come on earth, we pray.

Elizabeth Patton Moss

Words from *Twelve New World Order Hymns*, copyright 1958 by the Hymn Society of America. Used by permission.

This tune may also be used with "A hymn of glory let us sing," and "Before Jehovah's aweful throne."

Note that this hymntune is in the Dorian Mode, and observe the key signature: there are no B♭'s in this tune.

XIV. Trinity New

Metre: 6 10's

Note: Where there might be doubt or ambiguity as to which syllables go with which notes (as at *), bear in mind that *one* syllable is sung to all notes under the slur.

1. Thine are the souls, O God, our love would reach;
Thine is the good news word and act would teach;
Thine is the power for which we dare to ask
Who offer our devotion to thy task.
O Christ, the Word we strive to comprehend,
Be known to us as Teacher, Guide, and Friend.

2. May thy commission challenge soul and thought,
Until the peoples of the world be taught,
By every skill discipleship can use
And right example which the young may choose.
Thine is the promise to empower and gird,
Ours is the call to witness to the Word.

Elinor Lennen

This tune may also be used with "Eternal Ruler of the ceaseless round." This hymn should be sung in unison. On final stanza, organist may use tenor line as a descant, by playing it on prominent solo stop, 8′ and/or 4′, on separate manual.

XV. Poister

Metre: L. M. D. ("Long Metre Doubled"; 88. 88. 88. 88.)

1. All-knowing God, whose science charts
    The path and purpose of each star,
 Who showest man the laws and arts
    That whirl the mighty worlds afar;
 Endow the nations with new skill
    To use thy truth for larger good;
 Endow the people with new will
    To make the earth one neighborhood.

2. Almighty God, whose hand hath driven
    The ocean's fury, shaken hills,
 Yet patient strength to man hath given
    To break all shackles, right all ills;
 Embolden with thy might, we pray,
    The hosts who clear new roads to peace;
 Fulfill their vision of that day
    When terror, war, and strife shall cease.

3. All-loving God, who hatest naught
    Of thy creation's thousand forms,
 Who for man's fellowship hast sought
    Despite his spirit's rebel storms;
 Enlarge our love, strike down our hate;
    Thus may thy will be done on earth,
 And love fulfill in man and state
    The promise made at Jesus' birth.

William W. Reid

XVI. Alexander

Metre: 11 10. 11 10.

Stanzas 1, 2, 5 (Unison)

1. They come to me alert to life and eager,
   Reaching for truth and seeking for the way.
   I come to thee and ask for steady guidance:
   Teach me, O Lord, inspire the words I say.

2. They come to me with talents and with vigor
   To channel into skills, to do, to be.
   I bow my head, and ask thy help, thy wisdom,
   That I may challenge each with serving thee.

3. They come to me with needs and earnest questions,
   Each for himself, each different from the rest.
   I come to thee and ask for understanding;
   Enlighten me that I may meet each test.

4. They come to me, and all I have is little—
   They need so much, my best is far too small!
   I come to thee and bow in faith believing
   Thy boundless resource will augment my all.

5. They come to me; for this I needs must thank thee,
   For though unworthy, thou hast chosen me.
   I come to thee for cleansing; make me willing
   To be for them what thou wouldst have me be.

Lois Horton Young

Stanzas 3 and 4 (Harmony)

Chapter Sixteen

The Hymn: Free Harmonizations

Occasionally, such as on festivals of the Church Year, free harmonizations of one or more stanzas of hymns may be employed. These may be improvised, if the organist is sufficiently competent in extempore playing; or they may be written out beforehand. Some collections of free harmonizations are available, such as *Free Organ Accompaniments to Festival Hymns,* Vol. 1, and *Free Harmonizations of Twelve Hymn Tunes* published by Augsburg Publishing House. Not all hymns are adaptable to elaborate treatment, and free harmonizations should not be overdone; but a suitable hymn, appropriately handled, can offer meaningful inspiration to a congregation, revealing fresh insights into the melody, leading to bold singing, and becoming an exciting spiritual experience.

The free accompaniment should fit the words of the stanza in every case, being apt in mood and suitable stylistically to the character of the hymn. Sometimes merely a registration change, without chord changes or additional polyphony, is sufficient to point out anew the special meaning of a particular stanza or to enliven congregational singing.

Certain stanzas may be sung by men only, or women only; antiphonal effects between choir and congregation are also quite effective.

A well-written free harmonization should require no rehearsal, previous warning, or announcement to the congregation (at least if they have ever had any previous contact with such procedures); all stanza entrances should be so obvious that the congregation will know exactly when organ interludes are over and the next stanza is beginning. All settings should be obvious enough for the untrained congregation to follow without giving up in hopeless discouragement and frustration. The free accompaniments should not be so "contemporary" or dissonant that the congregation must stop singing; they should not be so "modern" that somewhat conservative congregations will be offended; yet they must be distinctive enough and vital enough to lend encouragement, lift hymn-singing out of the routine into the exalted, and renew inspiration for increased exhilaration of singing. Sometimes the free harmonization may grow progressively more "different" during four or five successive stanzas of a hymn, gradually preparing the congregation for more independence in singing.

Members of a congregation who make a practice of singing in harmony quickly learn to switch to unison when they hear a free accompaniment getting under way.

It should be noted that free hymn accompaniments may be used as unison anthems for children's choirs, for youth choirs, and for adult choirs.

Seasonal samples of free harmonizations follow. Flexibility should be the guiding principle in the use of these settings: stanzas may be repeated, alternated, shifted about, or omitted as desired.

St. Theodulph

(Valet will ich dir geben)

Metre: 76, 76. D

Paul Gerhardt, 1607-76
Tr. Composite

Melchior Teschner, 1584-1635

Organ Introduction.

Allegro moderato, with vigor

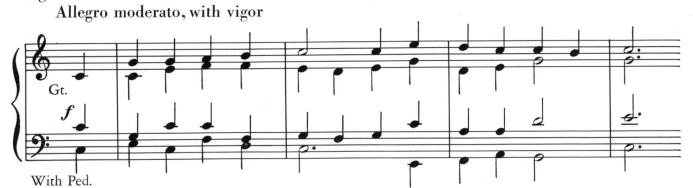

Gt.

f

With Ped.

St. 1: Harmony or unison

O how shall I re - ceive thee, how greet thee, Lord, a - right?

All na - tions long to see thee, My Hope, my heart's de - light!

O kin - dle, Lord most ho - ly, Thy lamp with - in my breast,

To do in spir - it low - ly All that may please thee best. Add Mixtures

St. 2: Men's voices, unison

Thy Zi - on palms is strew - ing, and branch-es fresh and fair;

My heart, its pow'rs re - new - ing, An an - them shall pre - pare.

My soul puts off her sad - ness Thy glo - ries to pro - claim;

With all her strength and glad - ness She fain would serve thy Name.

Both hands, full Swell

Ped. 16' to Swell

St. 3: All voices, unison

Gt. Trumpet, 8', *ff*, plus Gt. to Gt. 16' if effective; eighth notes slightly detached.

Love caused thine in - car - na - tion, Love brought thee down to me;

Sw. full, with 16', if not too thick; legato.

16', Principal chorus; Sw. to Ped.

Thy thirst for my sal - va - tion Pro - cured my li - ber - ty.

O love be - yond all tell - ing that led thee to em - brace,

In love all love ex - cell - ing, Our lost and fall - en race.

Both hands Great:

Slightly slower

St. 4: All voices, unison

Principal chorus with Mixtures

ff

Re - joice then, ye sad -

heart - ed, who sit in deep-est gloom, Who mourn o'er joys de-

part - ed And trem - ble at your doom, He who a - lone can

cheer you Is stand - ing at the door; He brings his pit - y

near you, And bids you weep no more. A - men.

Broaden

Vom Himmel hoch

Martin Luther, 1483-1546
Tr. Catherine Winkworth, 1829-1878

Martin Luther, 1483-1546

Metre: L.M.

Organ Introduction.

Moderato, firmly

Ped.

St. 1:

From heav'n a-bove to earth I come To bear good news to ev-'ry home; Glad

ti-dings of great joy I bring, Where - of I now will say and sing.

Sw. Flutes 8' and 2' or 8' and 4'

St. 2: Women's voices, unison

With quiet lyricism

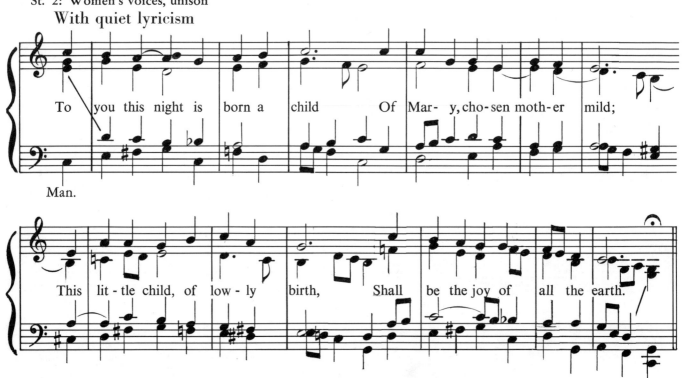

To you this night is born a child Of Mar-y, cho-sen moth-er mild;

Man.

This lit-tle child, of low-ly birth, Shall be the joy of all the earth.

136

Optional Registrations for Stanza 3:

1. { Both hands Gt. Principal chorus, **ff**   { R.H. Gt. Trumpet, 8', **ff**
   { Ped. 16', chorus, coupled   or 2. { L.H. Sw. chorus with Mixtures, **ff**
                                              { Ped. 16' to Sw.

St. 3: All voices, unison

Were earth a thou-sand times as fair, Be - set with gold and jew-els rare,

She yet were far too poor to be A nar-row cra-dle, Lord, to thee.

St. 4: Men's voices

Both hands Sw.,

Quietly

mp

Ah, dear-est Je-sus, Ho-ly Child, Make thee a bed, soft, un-de-filed,

without Ped.

With - in my heart, that it may be A qui-et cham-ber kept for thee.

137

St. 5: All voices, unison

Majestically

'Glo - ry to God in high-est heav'n, Who un - to man his Son hath giv'n,

ff

with Ped.

While an - gels sing with pi - ous mirth A glad new year to all the earth.

Epiphany

Dix
(Treuer Heiland)

St. 2 and 4: Women's voices

Metre: 77, 77, 77

A free harmonization for women's voices (suggested for the stanzas which begin "As with joyful steps they sped" and "Holy Jesus, every day").

Conrad Kocher, 1786-1872

Briskly

8' and 4'

without Ped.

O Filii et filiae

Metre: 8 8 8 4

Note: These free accompaniments may be used
for Stanzas 8 and 9 or any two or more Stanzas.

Jean Tisserand, D. 1494
Tr. John Mason Neale, 1818-1866

XV Century French Melody, Mode II

St. 8:

With energy and strength

*Optional Registration: Both hands on Gt., Full Chorus with Mixtures, *ff*; Ped. *ff* to Gt.

139

Full Organ

On this most ho- ly day of days, To God your hearts and voic- es raise In laud and ju- bi- lee and praise. Al - le- lu - ia!

Note that in SB&H and some other hymnals, the ascription (triple alleluia) which began this hymn is repeated at the end [not between stanzas, however]. It is therefore reproduced here.

Al- le- lu- ia, al - le- lu - ia, Al - - le- lu - - ia!

Wie schön leuchtet

Metre: Irregular

Philipp Nicolai, 1556-1608
Adapted and harm. by J. S. Bach, 1685-1750

Philipp Nicolai, 1556-1608

St. 1 and 2:
[Bach Harmonization]

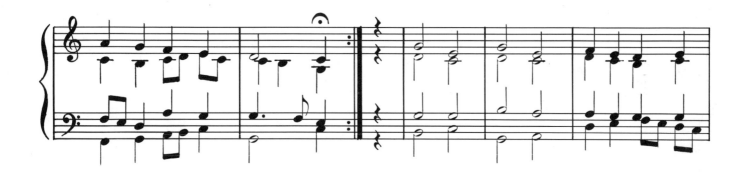

144

Nun danket alle Gott

Metre: 67, 67, 66, 66

Martin Rinkart, 1586-1649
Tr. Catherine Winkworth, 1829-1878

Johann Crüger, 1598-1662

Organ Introduction.

Majestically

Ped..

St. 1:

Now thank we all our God With

heart and hands and voic - es, Who won - drous things hath

done, In whom his world re - joic - es; Who,

from our moth - er's arms, Hath blessed us on our way With

count - less gifts of love, And still is ours to - day.

St. 2: { *Note:* It is suggested that St. 2 be sung by women's voices only. If, however, men also sing this stanza, play L.H. on separate manual with a light 16' stop in the combination.

O may this boun - teous God Through all our life be near

Man.

us, With ev - er joy - ful hearts And bless - ed peace to

cheer us; And keep us in his grace, And guide us when per -

plexed, And free us from all ills In this world and the next.

Wiltshire

Metre: C.M.

Nahum Tate, 1652-1715
Nicholas Brady, 1659-1726

George Thomas Smart, 1776-1867

St. 5:

Broadly

To Fa - ther, Son, and Ho - ly Ghost, The

God whom we a - dore, Be glo - ry, as it

was, is now, And shall be ev - er - more.

Chapter Seventeen

Stops and Registration

There are four broad classifications or categories of organ tone, excluding chimes and other percussions.

1. The principals, or diapasons, represent fundamental organ tone quality, usually produced by open metal pipes. Principals occur at a wide variety of pitches; many mutations, such as Twelfth 2⅔′ and Octave Quint 1⅓′, and most mixtures are of the principal family, because of the nature and construction of their pipes.

2. Flutes are the second category. Made either of wood or metal, and often capped, or stopped, they have less harmonic development (fewer upper partials) than principals, present a simpler, less vigorous tone, and are often, but not always, softer.

3. String pipes are almost always made of metal, and have a narrower gauging (smaller diameter) than principals, with a comparatively rich harmonic structure but with less development of the fundamental and other lower partials. Rarely very loud, they are somewhat "keener" than principals.

4. The reeds represent a broad and heterogeneous group. Construction of the reeds is different from that of the other groups: each reed pipe has a moving part—a small vibrating member in its base. The remainder of the pipe serves as resonator, controlling pitch and harmonic structure. Reeds are highly characteristic in sound, and some are quite loud.

The instructor may wish to demonstrate the appearance and physical characteristics of various pipes.

Some stops from the different categories above may be used together, but others do not blend well; they are not designed to do so. Experimentation and careful listening will help the student to develop a sensitive ear for stop combinations.

In an explanation of stops, it is more meaningful to discuss their roles in terms of a specific stoplist rather than to discuss them in the abstract. Therefore, one reasonably large specification has been chosen for evaluation and explanation. The instructor may wish to explain some of the terminology used and certain technical concepts presented.

First, the stoplist is given; descriptive and explanatory comments follow.

Stoplist
Boe Memorial Chapel
St. Olaf College, Northfield, Minnesota
(Organ by The Schlicker Organ Company)

Great	Positiv	Swell*	Pedal
16′ Gemshorn	8′ Holzgedeckt	16′ Quintadena	16′ Principal
8′ Principal	8′ Quintadena	8′ Principal	16′ Gemshorn (Great)
8′ Gemshorn	4′ Principal	8′ Rohrflöte	16′ Subbass
(from 16′)	4′ Rohrflöte	8′ Salicional	16′ Quintadena (Swell)
8′ Holzflöte	2′ Octave	8′ Celeste	8′ Octave
4′ Octave	2′ Nachthorn	8′ Dolce	8′ Gemshorn (Great)
4′ Spitzflöte	1⅓′ Larigot	4′ Octave	8′ Gedeckt
2⅔′ Quint	1′ Sifflöte	4′ Traversflöte	4′ Choral Bass
2′ Octave	II Sesquialtera	2⅔′ Nasat	4′ Gedeckt (from 8′)
VII Mixture	(Tenor C)	2′ Waldflöte	2′ Hohlflöte
IV Scharf	V Mixture	VI Mixture	III Rauschpfeife
8′ Trumpet	III Zimbel	16′ Contrafagott	IV Mixture
– Chimes	16′ Ranket	8′ Schalmei	32′ Contrafagott
(prepared)	8′ Krummhorn	4′ Clarion	(extension of
16′ Trompeta Real	4′ Regal	Tremolo	Swell)
(from 8′;	Tremolo		16′ Trombone
Tenor C)	– Zimbelstern	16′ ⎫	16′ Fagott (Swell)
8′ Trompeta Real	16′ Trompeta Real	4′ ⎭ Swell to Swell	16′ Ranket (Positiv)
4′ Trompeta Real	(from Great)		8′ Trumpet
(from 8′;	8′ Trompeta Real		4′ Clarion (from 8′)
49 notes:	(from Great)	*61-note chest	2′ Cornet (from 8′)
CC to c3	4′ Trompeta Real		8′ Great to Pedal
16′ ⎫	(from Great)		8′ Swell to Pedal
8′ ⎬ Swell to Great			8′ Positiv to Pedal
4′ ⎭	8′ ⎫		
	4′ ⎭ Swell to Positiv		
16′ ⎫			
8′ ⎭ Positiv to Great			

Accessories:

Manual Pistons: 5 Swell
     5 Great
     5 Positiv
     5 General
     1 General Cancel

Pedal Toe Studs: Generals 6-10
     5 Pedal
     1 General Cancel
     Sforzando, reversible

Swell pedal (Swell only is enclosed)
Crescendo pedal

Indicator lights: Crescendo; Sforzando

Notes: When one or more of the Positiv Trompetas Reales is drawn, an automatic Positiv Unison Off disconnects, internally, all other Positiv stops, which are then available only through couplers. The Positiv Trompetas Reales do not couple. The Great Trompeta Real 8′ *only* couples to Pedal.

Stop names and pitch characteristics of the above stoplist indicate that it is of contemporary German tendencies, leaning more toward the Classic school than the Romantic.

When an unfamiliar organ is being explored, the choruses are investigated first. A chorus is a combination of stops, usually of the Principal category and of different pitches, and normally on the same manual, which are an entity—that is, they are a group of stops designed and intended by the builder to work together as a cohesive, unified block of sound. Most choruses consist of a selected group of principal stops from 8' pitch up through one or more mixtures.

Referring to the stoplist above, the Great chorus should be analyzed first. It should be pointed out that in many organs there is a spatial different between the various divisions. That is, one can hear that the tone of each manual, and the pedal, comes from a different section of the organ. This is considered desirable and often is deliberately cultivated by the builder, rather than the policy of permitting all the sound to emanate from a large generalized location. In the interest of artistic integrity the distinct location of each division should be preserved when feasible, by avoiding unnecessary use of couplers.

The four basic members of the Great chorus are:

    8' Principal
    4' Octave
    2' Octave
  VII Mixture

The organ student could logically ask why these were not combined on one stop if they are a cohesive tonal entity designed to function as a unit. The answer is that, in the interest of flexibility and tonal variety, modifications are sometimes needed in the basic chorus. Since the 8', 4' and 2' are separately available, flexibility is possible. Of course there is no flexibility in the use of the VII Mixture; its components are voiced to be used together and there is no possibility of utilizing a few of its ranks without the remainder.

Listening to each of the above-listed chorus components separately, and then sampling them in combinations, will reveal how they complement each other, and together form a homogeneous tonal package. The foundation and the top, the 8' Principal and the VII Mixture, are the most important elements, for their voicing, once established by the builder, determines the voicing of the intermediate members of the chorus. Furthermore, the total tonal character of the Great chorus determines the nature of the Positiv, Swell, and Pedal choruses to a large degree, thus influencing to a significant extent the design of the entire instrument.

There are a number of modifications possible in the Great chorus:

    8' Gemshorn
    4' Octave   lightens the foundation of the ensemble
    2' Octave
  VII Mixture

    8' Principal
    4' Octave
  2⅔' Quint   makes the ensemble slightly richer and reedier
    2' Octave
  VII Mixture

    8' Principal
    4' Octave   for less volume and richness
    2' Octave

    8' Gemshorn
    4' Octave   for lucidity and transparency
    2' Octave

```
 8′ Principal
 4′ Octave          ⎫
 2′ Octave          ⎬  brightens the ensemble considerably
VII Mixture         ⎭
 IV Scharf

16′ Gemshorn
 8′ Principal       ⎫
 8′ Gemshorn        ⎪
 4′ Octave          ⎬  adds weight and dignity
2⅔′ Quint           ⎪
 2′ Octave          ⎭
VII Mixture
```

The Positiv chorus is examined next. The builder usually designs the chorus on the Positiv to be complementary to the Great chorus. As a rule, it is lighter and more lucid, with higher pitches represented. These two choruses can work in opposition to each other, as in concerto style; or the Positiv chorus can be used as a supplement to the Great by means of couplers, if desired.

```
 8′ Holzgedeckt
 4′ Principal
 2′ Octave
 1′ Sifflöte
 V Mixture
```

Before the nature of this Positiv chorus can be clearly understood, it should be noted that on this instrument, as on many from European traditions, there are differing pitch emphases on the various divisions. They are, in this case:

```
Pedal    16′ (and 32′)
Swell     8′ (and 16′)
Great     8′
Positiv   4′
```

Thus the basic pitch of the Positiv is 4′. For this reason, the 4′ Principal on the Positiv is called "Principal" rather than "Octave," and the first mutation member of the chorus is the 1⅓′ Larigot rather than a 2⅔′ Twelfth. One and one-third is the third harmonic of the 4′ pitch series. (The two pitch members of the Sesquialtera, 2⅔′ and 1⅗′, while lower than the Larigot, are voiced to belong to the cornet, not the chorus.) Furthermore, the Positiv Mixture is about one octave higher throughout its course than the Great VII Mixture.

However, even though the basic pitch emphasis of the Positiv is 4′, the performer must include an 8′ in combinations, or the Positiv would sound one octave too high. It should be observed that the builder is careful to provide only the 8′ Holzgedeckt (a flute) and the 8′ Quintadena (a flute-principal hybrid) on the Positiv: thus the organist is not permitted to destroy the 4′ emphasis by undergirding it with an 8′ Principal on this division. Either of the two eight-foot stops provided on the Positiv can serve as the basis of the chorus—the Holzgedeckt, having more body, is usually more suitable.

A number of modifications of the Positiv chorus are possible: for example, flutes may be substituted for the principals, or added to the chorus. It should be pointed out that the Zimbel, having a third among its three ranks (instead of the usual mixture disposition of octaves and fifths only) is actually a Terzzimbel, and although not particularly loud, is quite telling, even in full combinations. Its use should be somewhat limited since it is a special-purpose stop and has an extraordinarily high pitch band throughout its course.

One of the significant features of the Positiv division is the cornet (pronounced either kor-nay′ or kor-nett′). By tradition, the cornet is a combination of five ranks of flute timbre, consisting of the first five pitches of the overtone series, the 8′ being stopped pipes and the other four flutes open pipes. The cornet consists of:

8′ Holzgedeckt
4′ Rohrflöte
2′ Nachthorn
II Sesquialtera

This combination is designed for monody only (solo melodies), and is not intended for either harmonic or polyphonic use. Care should therefore be taken to withdraw it from full combinations, except in contemporary French homophonic music, in which it seems to be called for occasionally. The cornet has an unrivalled use as the solo combination in ornamented melodies of the Baroque Period.

The Swell chorus contains only three basic elements:

8′ Principal
4′ Octave
VI Mixture

When appropriate, the 2′ Waldflöte, which is metal, bright, and rich for a flute, may be added to the above entity.

The VI is a double-purpose Mixture: not only does it top the Swell principal chorus, but it is also voiced to blend with the reeds, serving almost as a 2′ reed. This fact is readily apparent if, starting with the Contrafagott, the following stops are added one at a time in the order indicated:

16′ Contrafagott
1. 8′ Schalmei
2. 4′ Clarion
3. VI Mixture

A mixture must be rich and fiery to contribute to a reed ensemble. Voiced for this purpose, the VI becomes quite prominent when used with the principals. In this case, some element of compromise is necessary when voicing the mixture.

There is no cornet on the Swell, and there is therefore no enclosed cornet on this organ. Possible substitutes for a cornet on the Swell would be:

8′ Rohrflöte
4′ Traversflöte
2⅔′ Nasat
2′ Waldflöte
        or:
8′ Rohrflöte
2⅔′ Nasat
2′ Waldflöte
        or:
8′ Rohrflöte
4′ Traversflöte
2⅔′ Nasat
Swell to Swell 4′

None of the above combinations, of course, contains one characteristic element of the cornet, the fifth harmonic: 1⅗′ Tierce.

The chorus of the Pedal division is:

16′ Principal
8′ Octave
4′ Choral Bass
IV Mixture

A great many modifications of the Pedal chorus are possible. It is a rather large and comparatively independent division.

The choruses having now been explored, the next step would be to set them all up, without couplers, and play passages changing back and forth among the manuals, to test them against each other. This procedure would reveal their relative volumes, pitch relationships, richness (such as predominance of fifths in the mixturework), and strength of fundamentals, or 8′ tone.

It is necessary to spend a great deal of time analyzing and evaluating the chorus structure of an organ. The construction, disposition, and tonal nature of the choruses are at the heart of an instrument: the choruses are the most widely used of all stop combinations; they are used in playing most of the literature of the organ and are indispensable in playing the works of Bach; they are used, with or without the mixtures, for hymn playing and much service playing.

Next the flutes are examined. Flutes serve many purposes: they provide contrast and variety against the principals; they serve as useful solo stops; the quieter flutes offer good accompanimental texture; they serve admirably at many pitches and in many combinations in trio work. On this instrument, there are at least 8′ and 4′ members of the flute category represented on every division, including the Pedal. There is a wide range of brightness and mellowness. Ordinarily, one checks the flutes for the interesting acoustical quality of "chiff" or "chirp." Acousticians call this physical phenomenon "spinach." Unless it is taken out in voicing at the factory, an initial transient is produced by some pipes for a fraction of a second. This sound may be either spurious or a harmonic overtone. It may be removed, or partially eliminated, by the process called nicking the pipes. Some organ builders, preferring bland tone, carefully "refine-out" virtually all the chiff from their instruments. Such builders consider initial transients rough, uncouth, and undesirable. Other builders with a Classic viewpoint cultivate chiff, considering it useful, animated, and dynamic. It tends to accentuate rhythmic vitality through its incisiveness and contributes charm and vigor to melodies and polyphony.

Chiff is not, however, limited to flutes, although it is most commonly observed among them. On this instrument the Great Gemshorn, a quiet principal, and the strings have a certain amount of chiff.

It should be noted that although organ builders use such descriptive terms as "flute," "string," and "trumpet," the organ is by no means an imitative instrument. The fact that certain kinds of tone call to mind similarities with orchestral timbres is more accidental than intentional: organs make no attempt to be a one-man band or orchestra, and no such claim is made for them. The organ is intended to sound only like itself. This is a positive rather than a negative approach, since the instrument which attempts to imitate all others is apt to lack any individual character or aesthetic honesty of its own.

An examination of the strings on this instrument reveals again a Classic trend: there are few strings, and the category is represented only on one manual. These strings are located on the Swell. Their placement on the Swell is valid for two reasons: first, crescendi and diminuendi are quite effective on the strings because of their overtone structure; second, much of the music which calls for strings dates from the Romantic Period, the Nineteenth Century, which also requires that they be under expression. The three strings on this instrument are the Salicional, the Celeste, and the Dolce.

There is a proportionately large number of reeds on this organ, and they appear at a variety of pitches. The Great 8′ Trumpet, a fiery French reed, is admirable for solos and is also good in ensembles. The Swell reed chorus of three members is French, in spite of their German nomenclature. The Schalmei can be used as a small Trompette in solo work; and it greatly enriches the texture in ensembles. The Swell 4′ Clarion is *fortissimo*, and approximately equivalent in volume and harmonic development to the Great Trumpet. The Positiv reeds, on the other hand, are short resonator German reeds, highly distinctive in character and with a touch of humor. They are much softer, and are not always used in ensemble work. Their solo qualities, however, are exceptional. The Pedal has a large reed chorus in number, volume, and pitch representation. The 16′ Trombone is a voice of such power as to permit it to serve almost as a bass for the Trompeta Real.

The Trompeta Real, a special-purpose reed rank mounted visibly and almost horizontally is, as would be expected, the loudest single voice on the instrument. Its almost incredible richness is demonstrated by the fact that a single pipe will be found to have 65 or more overtones by actual electronic analysis. Such special sounds should be used infrequently as their effectiveness is lessened by overuse. They should be limited to occasions of pomp and ceremony and the like. This is not to imply that they are merely unmusical gadgets and a waste of the organbuilder's art. They are rather quite legitimate—and, indeed, glorious—and are most certainly intended to be used—but sparingly.

How much should the couplers be used on this organ? A good general rule is, the larger the instrument, the less necessity for utilization of couplers. But in practice couplers ought to be used whenever it is necessary to combine components from two or more divisions to achieve the exact tonal combination desired. The conscientious organist tries at the same time to avoid sacrificing the integrity of divisions.

Chapter Eighteen

Ornamentation

Ornamentation requires serious study and thought on the part of organ students, since organists perform so much of the literature of the Baroque Period, during which time ornaments were a featured part of performance.

Any systematic investigation of ornamentation requires much individual help from the instructor, as well as careful reading in the literature. Although an instruction book cannot take the place of an instructor, some basic principles are offered here.

Ornamentation exists for the purpose of enriching and enlivening music; it was originally improvised, and left up to the discretion of the performer.

Gradually the improvised melodic fragments inserted by interpreters became formalized and stereotyped, and various signs and symbols arose which stood for certain melodic patterns and formulae.

Later composers began to write out the exact notation they desired—there was a trend toward exact precision of notation—and extempore ornamentation by the performer was discouraged. By 1800, most improvised ornaments had disappeared.

In the Baroque Period (ca. 1600-1750), however, discretionary improvisation played a large part in performance.

It is suggested that, in general, the organ student observe the following guiding principles:

1. Ornaments may be added at will, provided all is done within the taste and style of the period. They may occasionally be altered, or one ornament may be substituted for another (for example, a turn may sometimes be used instead of a trill).

2. It is often appropriate to add an ornament to the penultimate note (the next-to-last note) of a phrase, provided this procedure sounds aesthetically right.

3. The beginner should normally limit improvised added ornaments to the trill, the short trill, the mordent and the turn. (Note that the appearance of a few ornaments on a page does not preclude the use of additional ones. Those which do appear may be interpreted as suggestions or hints as to what the composer considers logical for that passage.)

4. In a fugue subject, any ornaments which occur during the earlier part of the statement and are featured melodically should usually be repeated, unchanged, each time the subject enters. However, most ornamentation in fugue subjects is cadential (occurring toward the end of the statement) and may be altered or omitted at subsequent appearances of the subject. Do not underestimate the musical and technical capabilities of the pedals. Trills in the pedal are quite possible and should not be neglected, although it is undeniably true that very fast ornaments must be slowed down or omitted.

5. By the same token, ornaments may be changed at repeated passages.

As to performance, musicologists do disagree somewhat as to nomenclature and methods of execution. Most recent research indicates the following interpretations as authentic:

1. Mordent($\text{\textit{\textbf{w}}}$): play the principal note on the beat, then the lower auxiliary, then the principal note (with lower note in the key of the moment unless a chromatic alteration is indicated). Occasionally, but more rarely, the mordent may be executed with five or seven or more notes, always alternating between the principal and the lower auxiliary. When several mordents occur in close proximity, some performers execute the first as a three-note ornament and the others with varied numbers of alternations.

2. Trill ($\text{\textit{w}}$, $\text{\textit{ww}}$ or $\textit{tr}$): This ornament always begins with the upper auxiliary on the beat. The ornament may consist of four or six or more notes. The performer is free to end this ornament with a "termination" (which consists of the lower auxiliary and a return to the principal note); or the composer may write out the termination or a pattern substituting for it. As to rhythm, the trill may be either free or metrical, at the discretion of the performer and depending somewhat on the context. When the free trill is used, professional organists generally begin it slowly and then accelerate to more rapid alternations; they usually ritard slightly at the conclusion of the trill (these tempo changes naturally occur only if the trill is reasonably long). When the metrical trill is used, it should, as a normal procedure, be executed in notes half the value of the most rapid note generally found in the texture.

3. Turn (∞) consists of four notes, the upper auxiliary, the principal note, the lower auxiliary, and a return to the principal note.

4. There are a number of other ornaments, such as the appoggiaturas from above and below, which may be found described in various texts and articles. Bibliographical information is given at the end of this chapter.

Bear in mind that manuscripts (including Bach's) were often hastily written. Composers were therefore unavoidably, but regrettably, careless and inconsistent. As regards the interpretation of any given symbol found on a page, the best indication as to the composer's intent is where the sign occurs in the music, and the context.

Because of the inherent flexibility of ornamentation, time values in the illustrations below should be interpreted as approximate. Ornaments should be played with freedom and an air of improvisation.

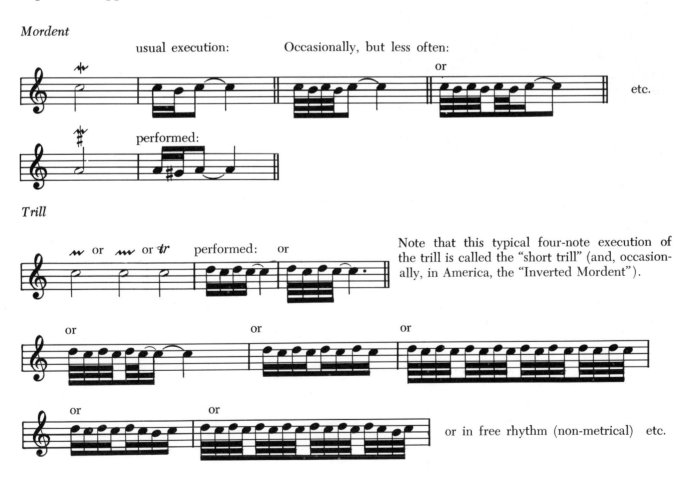

Mordent

usual execution: Occasionally, but less often: or   etc.

performed:

Trill

$\text{\textit{w}}$ or $\text{\textit{ww}}$ or $\textit{tr}$ performed: or

Note that this typical four-note execution of the trill is called the "short trill" (and, occasionally, in America, the "Inverted Mordent").

or   or   or

or   or

or in free rhythm (non-metrical)   etc.

157

Turn

When passages like the following occur: The note marked (A) should always be ornamented.

For example:

For further information, consult:

Aldrich, Putnam. *Ornamentation in J. S. Bach's Organ Works.* New York: Coleman-Ross Company, Inc., 1950.

Aldrich, Putnam. "On the Interpretation of Bach's Trills," *The Musical Quarterly,* Vol. XLIX, No. 3 (July, 1963). New York: G. Schirmer, Inc.

Apel, Willi, Ed. "Ornamentation." *Harvard Dictionary of Music,* pp. 542-546. Cambridge, Massachusetts: Harvard University Press, 1950.

Chapter Nineteen

Legato and Staccato Styles

Most authorities consider the legato style the proper basic technique of organ playing, and the properly-trained organ student will have a good legato technique.

However, some organ repertoire requires a detached or staccato touch. Most of the old masters of organ literature did not indicate in their manuscripts their desires in touch, phrasing, or articulation. It is occasionally wise to experiment with various touches to see if the ear selects something other than legato as musically preferable and stylistically reasonable.

Play the melodic fragment below in the various ways indicated. Then experiment with additional phrasings and choose the one you consider best for this particular passage. Then apply this experimental approach to organ compositions, especially of the Baroque Period. This procedure will help you to develop sensitivity to the wide variety of articulations possible and available for your selection and utilization.

1. All legato

2. All detached (semi-staccato)

3. All staccato

4. Inner-phrased or articulated

5. Inner-phrased

6. Inner-phrased

Chapter Twenty

The Organist in Church Work;
Service Playing

Participation in the musical program and activities of a church is a privilege and an honor, and should never be considered merely a routine task or a stepping-stone to a "better profession" such as concert work.

Since church work represents a high calling, requiring a devotional approach and sound spiritual attitudes, the person in the profession solely for financial considerations should leave church work and find another profession. It must be said that an organist should not seek an affiliation with a denominational group unless he can view its dogmas, credos, ritual, and methods of worship with sympathy. This does not mean that he must join that particular church, nor does it imply that he must subscribe explicitly to all facets of its doctrine; but he must be willing, privately in his own mind, to support its teachings, giving his cooperation freely in the worship endeavors.

The organ plays a varied role in worship, and can assist in establishing and sustaining attitudes and moods conducive to worship. Sometimes the organ represents the Holy Spirit, speaking with commanding authority, great boldness, and tongues of flame, as it were. At other times the organ speaks on behalf of a humble congregation, with quiet awe and reverent devotion. The seasons demand flexibility of sound and style: in typical protestant churches, for example, Christmas evokes wonder, praise, and adoration; Lent probes the sinfulness of mankind, with quiet agony and melancholy; Easter fills the air with overwhelming joy at the Resurrection and the promise of immortality through Jesus Christ.

As to the selection of organ music, it is desirable and necessary that in corporate worship a unified service be presented, in which the words spoken by the minister, the hymns sung by the congregation, the anthems performed by the choirs, and the prelude, offertory, and postlude played by the organist will focus the attitudes and thoughts of the worshipping congregation on the specific message of the day.

While certain portions of the service remain constant and unchanged throughout the year, other elements, which are called the Propers, do change. Examples of the Propers for the day are the Introit, Gradual, Collect, Lesson, Epistle, and Gospel. Through these Propers and their subject matter we are able to derive the specific emphasis of the Sunday or particular day of the Christian year to which our attention is being drawn.

Some might wonder why it is necessary to stress somewhat different subject matter at each service, since there is basically one Christian message and it would be beneficial to dwell upon it continually. But there are, of course, so many facets to the Christian faith and numerous attendant doctrines that it is not possible to examine them all at once. Therefore the Christian year, an annual rotating calendar system, permits us to center our thoughts on a few portions at a time, probing depths of meaning, applying implications to our own lives, and contemplating great truths at a comparatively leisurely pace.

It has long been accepted that the arts can contribute greatly to the impact of a corporate worship experience. Music can assist greatly in establishing a mood or atmosphere, and this task can be accomplished rather quickly, if necessary, with just a few "broad strokes." The opposite is also true: just a few measures of tasteless or inappropriate music can completely shatter a mood of sacred contemplation.

The effectiveness of music in playing this role of mood-setting, or attitude establishing, is due to associations, recollections, and a complex structure of conditioned and learned responses to stimuli which have developed through many years. The unique efficacy of music to achieve this is the result of its ability to mean different things to different people, speaking personally and intimately to each since it is essentially unspecific. Thus it can become a powerful influence on each separate individual. Musicians, however, do not consider themselves applied psychologists, but they rather approach these matters from the spiritual point of view, bearing also in mind many aesthetic and artistic considerations.

It must be clearly understood that music cannot represent a concrete fact or tell a specific story. For example, the organist could not state, musically, "Thou hast kept the good wine until now"—a phrase which occurs in one of the Propers for the Second Sunday after the Epiphany. Nevertheless, it is necessary that the organist relate, as much as possible, the musical portions of the service to the themes and topics of the day. The organist must cooperate with the minister and choir director so that maximum unity be achieved in the worship service.

As to the selection of suitable organ music such as preludes, offertories, and postludes, *A Guide to Music for the Church Year*, Augsburg Publishing House, 1962, will be found to be very helpful. It contains lists of organ music, as well as anthems, appropriate and suitable for the various Sundays and other special days of the Christian year.

Some hymnals provide helps, such as the Liturgical Index (pp. 1004-1007) in the Lutheran *Service Book and Hymnal*, giving hymns related to the Propers for the day, as follows: procession, Introit, Psalm paraphrase, Epistle, Gradual and Gospel.

Many publishers of collections of organ preludes, offertories, and postludes are now providing helpful topical indices which indicate seasonal appropriateness of the various selections.

As to playing the liturgical portions of the service, such as the Kyrie, Gloria in Excelsis, Nunc Dimittis, and others, there seem to be five schools of thought, each point of view having its adherents:

1. All the sung portions of the liturgy should be sung in unison, unaccompanied, by the congregation. The role of the organ is to provide preliminary pitches.

2. The liturgy should be sung in unison by the congregation, and the organ should accompany it unobtrusively at the unison, with no chords or other implications of harmony.

3. The congregation should sing the liturgy in unison, and the organ should provide chordal accompaniment, but the tonal quality or timbre of the accompaniment should be light and unobtrusive (such as Gedeckt 8' and Prestant 4'); no pedal or other thickening textures should be used.

4. The congregation may sing the liturgy in harmony, as desired, except where unison is specifically directed; the organ assumes a dominant role of leadership, using pedals, deeper rich tones, and full principal chorus with mixtures occasionally.

5. The liturgy is sung in unison by the congregation. An accompaniment of harmonic or polyphonic nature is improvised by the organist, preferably different each Sunday, so that continual freshness and vitality are preserved; the organ is dynamic and assertive.

The writer finds certain unique advantages in each of the five procedures outlined above, as well as inescapable flaws in each. Most organists have undoubtedly experimented with several different approaches; it is best not to make a final decision which excludes all interpretations but one. Different seasons and situations require new and different treatments.

As to the mechanics of playing the service, *The Organist's Edition of the Liturgy*, Augsburg Publishing House, 1963, is recommended to all Lutheran organists. The spiral-bound book lies flat, it is easy to read, and there are no page-turning requirements in the middle of a chant.

Chapter Twenty-One

Playing on Two Manuals with One Hand

It is sometimes necessary for one hand to play notes simultaneously on two keyboards.

1 Right hand drill, two manuals.   Practice very slowly at first.

Swell, *mf*, Reed, 8′
Great, *p*, Flutes 8′ and 4′

Soprano voice on Swell.

Alto voice on Great.

2 Left hand drill, two manuals.   Tenor voice on Great, and bass voice on Swell.
Practice also gliding with the thumb.

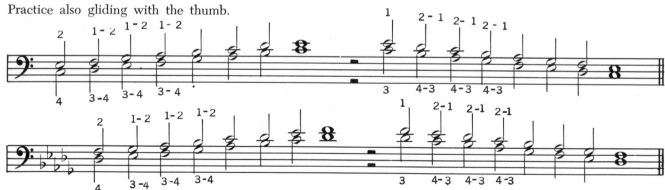

3 "Alternate thumbs" drill.

Soprano and tenor on Swell, *mp*, Flutes 8′ and 4′
Alto on Great, *mf*, Principal 8′

For performance: alternate thumbs on Great; change fingers as necessary, using third and fourth fingers, on Swell, both hands.

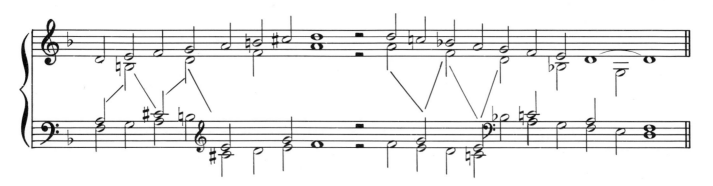

4 Drill in a more complex design

Practice hands separately first

While continuing to play on Great, change Sw. to Reed, 4', or 4' and 2', *ff—No 8' on Sw.*

Add mixture, *f*, to Gt.

Great

Sw. (4' only or 4' + 2' *ff*)—keep baritone voice on Swell.

(Gt.)

(Sw.)

164

165

166

Chapter Twenty-Two

Improvisation for the Beginner

Of all serious musicians, organists are among the few who are commonly expected to improvise competently in public. The student should begin early to develop this skill. Here are a few informal practical suggestions, rather than theoretical rules. The teacher may offer guidance if some terms used below are unfamiliar to the student.

There are two kinds of improvisation:

I. Service type, consisting of extempore music used under the following circumstances and in similar situations:

1. Free harmonizations of one or more stanzas of a hymn

2. Appropriate music while congregation partakes of communion

3. Introductions to anthems (endeavoring to maintain the style of the choral selection to follow)

4. Interludes (sometimes modulatory) between stanzas of a hymn

5. Quiet music while ushers are seating latecomers (but meaningless wanderings should be avoided)

6. Occasionally, brief passages of background music when service is broadcast, while minister is moving about or when there is a temporary awkward silence. Bear in mind, however, that it is not always necessary for the organist to fill lulls in the service with sound: sometimes a high peak of the worship experience occurs during a period of absolute silence.

II. Formal, or concert type:

1. Elaborate and extended preludes, offertories or postludes, using a definite musical form or design

2. Recital improvisations, usually based on one or more themes submitted by the audience, often a complex multi-movement design at a very advanced level.

As a practice aid, elementary improvising may be broken down into four elements which may be practiced somewhat separately, although they interact and none can be isolated from the others in the strictest sense. The four elements are: 1. Tonality; 2. Harmony; 3. Melody; and 4. Polyphony. After the student has become somewhat familiar with these four elements, he may begin to combine them formally in small compositional designs. The writer suggests that the elements listed above be practiced in the order indicated, although some authorities advocate practicing melody and polyphony before harmony; others prefer that all elements be approached at the same time.

Here are suggested steps.

I. Practice tonality

1. Practice, on piano, all major and minor scales daily. This familiarizes the mind and fingers with the various keys.

2. Practice establishing all keys, major and minor (called "clinching the key"). This and all succeeding steps should be done at the organ; pedals should be used as soon as the student achieves reasonable

facility. The following chord progressions are suggested for clinching:

a. I, IV, V, I; also I, IV, V⁷, I
b. I, II⁶, V, I; also I, II⁶, V⁷, I
c. I, II⁷, V, I; also I, II⁷, V⁷, I
d. I, II$_5^6$, V, I; also I, II$_5^6$, V⁷, I
e. I, IV⁷, V, I; also I, IV⁷, V⁷, I
f. I, VI, II⁶ or IV, V, I; also I, VI, II⁶ or IV, V⁷, I

Typical examples of the above and similar progressions are illustrated below in major and minor keys. Other inversions (such as I⁶) and passing tones may be used freely, as well as any other devices of artistic merit.

168

The above are basically cadence formulae. They are easy, and should be practiced until they become second nature and can be played automatically, while you are thinking of something else. Avoid using the same positions, same soprano melody, and same bass progressions each time you practice these exercises in different keys. Continually shift to varying inversions, positions, and melodic lines. As a normal procedure, utilize steps rather than skips in progressions, and when convenient observe contrary motion between soprano and bass.

II. Practice harmony

1. Play a series of eight chords in each key. Give each chord one or two beats. The chords must be organized so that the last chord returns home to the tonic and sounds aesthetically logical. Maintain three or four voices, at least at first, avoiding adding notes indiscriminately to random chords. Try to think in a linear manner. *Note:* do not neglect the minor mode. Give special attention to the musical possibilities of the chromatic alterations of the 6th and 7th degrees of the scale in minor. Playing in the minor mode, although it is somewhat difficult, brings a special reward: it usually sounds more "professional" —less trite—than the major mode.

Examples:

2. Next, try a series of eight chords with the addition of one passing tone or other additional note between each chord. Then try a triplet figure between each basic chord.

170

3. Next practice doing several things at once to force yourself to think on several levels simultaneously and to learn to function "semi-automatically" at the keyboard. The best device for developing this complex skill is the "ramble," which may be explained as follows: begin to improvise slowly in an easy key, using right hand and pedal. With the left hand, gradually add all the stops from softest to loudest, and then reverse this procedure, retiring the stops from loudest to softest. Repeat this a number of times, in increasingly difficult keys. This training maneuver makes no pretense of being artistic, but is nevertheless quite useful.

III. Practice melody

Attempt to create unaccompanied tunes, at first on a very modest basis. As it becomes possible, achieve rhythmic vitality by utilizing a variety of note values (rather than, say, all quarter notes). Bear in mind that the listener usually hears implied harmony in unaccompanied melodies. Chapters 2, 3, 5, 6 and 7 of this manual offer some examples of unaccompanied melodic lines.

IV. Practice polyphony

Polyphony is the musical art of combining two or more rhythmically and melodically independent lines. Begin to develop this skill by adding an additional melodic line to the melody of familiar hymntunes. Use one manual or two as appropriate. Although it is quite difficult at first, attempt to improvise a few canons, in which one voice imitates, literally, the other voice. ("Rounds" are good examples of the canonic technique.) Later, as you develop contrapuntal skill, attempt a few three-voice designs, or trios, for right hand, left hand, and pedal. You may begin development of this skill by slowly playing the soprano and bass lines of familiar hymns while the left hand improvises a free tenor or alto melodic line. Chapters 8 and 9 of this book offer some polyphonic illustrations.

V. Practice larger designs

1. Practice *devices* (such as suspensions, passing tones, ornaments, chromatic modulations). Here is an example of suspensions:

2. Practice *patterns* (such as pizzicato bass, chorale style, solo pedal cadenza, an occasional atonal design, etc.)

3. Practice *forms* and *structures* (such as simple aria da capo, scherzo, toccata, passacaglia, fughetta, etc.)

Students who are so inclined should feel free to move away from traditional, "triadic" designs, such as the illustrations given in this chapter, and experiment with chords and structures built on seconds, fourths, and sevenths, and other contemporary idioms. Most instructors do suggest, however, that it is often wise to master familiar keyboard territory before setting out to conquer more hazardous regions.

In conclusion it may be said that all improvisation is a search for beauty—and the writer wishes you successful hunting in that search. Use any rules of harmony as guide lines, if you know them; but do not be a slave to any petty regulations. Occasionally be daring. It should be noted that it is pointless to compare good improvising with the best "written down" or composed music by master composers. You may never improvise anything comparable with a Bach chorale; to demand such an accomplishment of yourself would be unreasonable. Improvisation has its own aims, purposes and goals, and well performed, it can be an artistically ennobling and spiritually satisfying experience, supremely suited to the occasion and eminently pleasing.

Left Hand Carrying Three Legato Voices

Watch voice leading carefully: practice left hand alone first, being sure that it is playing three notes, but no more than three, at all times.

Adagio (♩=48 to 52)

R. H.: *mp*, Flutes 8′ and 4′

L. H.: Flute 8′ and Salicional 8′, *p* (Both hands molto legato)

Pedal: Gedeckt, 16′, *p*, coupled to L. H. manual

Chapter Twenty-Four

On Teaching

Organists often find that, in connection with church positions, they have opportunities to give organ instruction to choir members and other interested church personnel.

Here are a few informal remarks and suggestions to those organ students who may some day have a class of their own organ pupils.

Most instructors learn to teach by the actual process of teaching, rather than by being told how to do so. Furthermore, most instructors teach the way they were taught, rather than the way they were told to teach. It is virtually impossible to tell another person how to teach, because each of his pupils must be taught differently. All pupils are individuals with differing backgrounds, experience, and weaknesses; all have different aims and goals; each learns at a somewhat different rate of growth and accomplishment. It is therefore not at all necessary, or even advisable, that all students receive the same order of assignments, or the same compositions to work on. Each pupil requires a different approach. Therefore an identical teaching routine for all, involving the same exercises, drills, and advice, is arbitrary and fruitless.

Do not move too slowly to new skills, and techniques. The young amateur is stifled by exercises and repetitive drill beyond that which is necessary. He needs new experiences for renewed motivation. Some inexperienced teachers make the mistake of advancing their students too slowly. They expect great musical subtlety and artistry on each line of the beginners' method book. However, most students cannot learn satisfactorily without a continual sense of achievement, progress, and accomplishment. The sensitive teacher encourages fairly rapid growth without spending, at first, too great a proportion of time on routine drill. Yet at the same time it is sometimes imperative for the teacher to spend a great deal of time on some one isolated problem if it is clearly indicated to be a weakness or bad habit on the part of a particular student.

After hearing a student perform a composition at a lesson, let him know where he stands in regard to level of accomplishment: rather than merely saying, "let's hear it again next week," discuss and comment upon his playing with specific suggestions as much as possible. Point out weaknesses or irregularities in rhythm, perhaps, or phrasing, or tempo, or deficiencies in stylistic interpretation. Furthermore, when calling the student's attention to a problem, suggest to him procedures for correcting or alleviating the difficulty: students sometimes do not know actual methods of eliminating problems through correct practice. Teachers should not take too much for granted on the erroneous assumption that their pupils have already achieved self-discipline and professional attitudes toward practice.

Call each student by name, and take a genuine interest in him and in his artistic growth. Students are quick to sense when lessons have become a routine and boring task to the teacher. Poor attitudes on the part of the instructor lead quickly to loss of incentive and motivation on the part of the average pupil. When it is appropriate, spend extra time with students away from the studio, providing and participating in social events when it is feasible to do so.

Musical performance is a subtle art, and the teaching of various aesthetic refinements requires close rapport and a high order of empathy. The growth of sensitive artistry takes place only under ideal conditions, fostered by a comfortable feeling of mutual understanding, sympathy, and cordial and unstrained relations. The teacher should take the first step of showing the initiative of interest and warmth toward the student (but do not overdo it). Do not be afraid of being hurt (some students will resist you, and persons who are afraid of being hurt do not extend themselves, but wear a protective shell, so that they cannot be attacked easily). Yet most great teachers are accessible—and, of course, that makes them vulnerable, too. But do not worry if the students seem not to respond: they may wish very much to respond, but fear you, or not know how to be demonstrative.

Of course no matter how much you are trying to develop cordial relations with your pupils, you must be truthful and frank about their progress and development, not hesitating to speak severely if they are not practicing adequately or growing as you feel they should. However, be cautious about uttering categorical predictions, either good or bad, about their future as professional organists. Sometimes a very "slow starter" who seems almost hopeless for the first few months develops gradually into an organist of taste, talent, and competence; while occasionally a beginner whose first few lessons seem like brilliant bursts of budding genius withers quickly.

Do not hesitate to assign your students compositions occasionally which you yourself have not studied; once in a while assign a piece with which you are totally unfamiliar, if it seems right for the next stage in the student's development. Even though you may not know the piece, you can still correct note and phrasing errors by merely observing the page and checking on accuracy. Also, because of your wider experience, you can give the student helpful ideas on the composer, his style, fitness of interpretation, and hints on registration. If the composition is totally unfamiliar to you, you will of course be unable to help with fingering or pedaling of difficult passages, but the student often needs the experience of working out such things independently anyway.

Avoid being jealous of your students; encourage their strongest points. You may discover that many of them develop some one technique or another which they handle very well, even more adroitly or competently than yourself: one may have a distinctive knack of fitness in registration; another an immaculate pedal technique; or another a superb control over staccato notes. These represent in no way a threat to you. The fearful, lazy, or weak teacher succumbs to the temptation of playing down and "debunking" students' superior attributes if he himself cannot perform as well. He cannot permit them to surpass him in any way, and keeps them on easy music or exercises, not allowing them to play the pieces he is having trouble with, or not permitting them to play his "specialty" repertoire, for fear that they will play it better. The wise teacher is honest with himself and his deficiencies. This is not to say that he deliberately reveals his inadequacies to students: some students, being yet children, do not understand the virtue of true humility and are apt to accept a teacher on his own estimate of his worth. The teacher's obligation is to make his pupils the finest musicians possible, and to assist them in rising to their highest potential.

Play often for your students. Setting a good example, more than much explanation and discussion, reveals interpretation and style, and acquaints them with repertoire. Have your students play often for each other. Performing for other students is a good incentive to practice; the element of competition (if handled wisely) can prod students to better effort and achievement; and performances by your students are an extension of your teaching, revealing your ideas on pieces which all might not have the opportunity of studying with you. Your best students will actually compete primarily with you, either consciously or unconsciously. You are their best example (sometimes, indeed, you are the only professional performing organist they have heard). Some of your finest students will confidently hope and expect to surpass you as a performer in a few short years. Although you are their idol in many ways, they nevertheless quickly learn all your flaws and imperfections only too well.

When it is feasible, avoid assigning all your advanced students *any* of the same pieces. There is far more than enough organ literature to go around. When everyone in an organ class is doing the same Franck Choral, the same Bach Prelude and Fugue, and the same contemporary composition, all using the same registration and fingering (written in diligently from the teacher's copy), the group begins to suffocate for lack of fresh ideas and vision.

It is important to recognize when a pupil has learned much or most of what you have to offer; the time may have come to send him to advanced work with a master teacher. Relinquishing a superior student for his own good and future development is one of the most difficult things we teachers must face.

It is recommended that all your students, even the elementary ones, once they have passed the method stage, be working on at least one composition from each of the following categories at all times:

A. Pre-Bach and/or Handel

B. J. S. Bach

C. The Romantic Period

D. Contemporary French

E. Contemporary German

A few very easy compositions may be found in each of the five categories, of course.

Students may have many questions concerning speed in organ playing. The normal rule regarding maximum tempo for clarity is simply this: play at a tempo only so fast as to permit the individual notes to be heard distinctly. However, sometimes the spirit of a composition requires a more rapid tempo. In certain cases, if the individual notes are somewhat blurred, it does not matter: the composition does not suffer because its strength lies in general impact rather than in specifics. As an analogy, envision a mob of people, furiously bent upon some action. The situation bears an intense emotional impact, even though you cannot understand a word anyone says. On the other hand, certain compositions are cheapened and made to seem insignificant by too fast a tempo.

Advise your students to use "dead keyboard" or silent keyboard practice occasionally. This procedure is especially useful in working on trios. Have them practice a trio with one, two or all three parts on silent keyboards.

Occasionally a student may ask why you play a piece one way but permit a student to play the same composition in a different manner or style. Explain that there may be more than one suitable way of interpreting a composition musically. Music is an art, and the arts must never be confused with the sciences (where it is sometimes found that there is only one correct answer to a problem). In the arts there are often many possible solutions to the same aesthetic problem; however, occasionally something is right under some circumstances and wrong under others. Should a painter use blue and purple together? It depends. Should an organist combine string, flute, and reed stops? It depends. The author would like to coin a phrase at this point: "consistency is the refuge of petty minds." In other words, do a thing differently when the occasion requires a fresh approach.

One measure of the greatness of a teacher is his skill in handling the student who is a "rebel." The rebel challenges established traditions and opinions, and may openly or covertly oppose his teacher's policies and convictions. However, such an iconoclast, if he is diligent, sincere and conscientious, offers a definite contribution to a class of organ students. Use care in reining him in, to avoid stifling a possible creative and enterprising individualist. His ideas may be daring and bold, and also foolish. Try to curb his more extreme follies without upsetting his adventurous temperament. He is quite difficult to teach because he will never accept merely your word or your authority: you must explain to him *why* things must be so, technically and artistically. Of course, if he is a rebel merely because some deep-seated inferiority demands a desperate attempt at recognition and self-assertion, he is not a true intellectual rebel at all, but rather a frightened and neurotic child who must be treated in an entirely different manner. There is, regrettably, another kind of individual who assumes the guise of the rebel: the student who finds it easier to rebel against authority than to attempt, under authority, to accomplish anything truly creative. Such a person disagrees with the teacher as an excuse to avoid having to do any work under the pretext that the assignment is wrong or inept. But the genuine rebel may be right in challenging both us as teachers and our traditions. Certainly he helps cause us to re-think some of our preconceptions and established notions.

The student or teacher who is continually critical, harshly and destructively, of his fellows and colleagues is apt to indicate by his attitude that he is insecure and inadequate himself: he attempts to undermine the accomplishments of others as compensation for being unable to elevate himself along legitimate and creative channels. Thus it gives him a feeling of superiority to point out any shortcomings he can detect in others, to divert attention from his own shortcomings which may be legion. The person who is secure and professionally competent can afford to be generous in praise when it is deserved, and charitable, gentle, and just in criticism when it can be offered wisely and constructively.

Avoid at all costs the temptation to "use" your organ students to further your own ambitions or reputation. This tendency, which can endanger the future career of the student, takes several forms: giving him music that is too difficult; forcing public performances too soon; choosing a repertoire of "spectacular" compositions without a solid foundation in the standard classics of organ literature. Students gradually discover that they are being exploited, and their desire to please their instructor is considerably lessened. The teacher's reputation will be more permanently enhanced by genuine interest in the students and little thought for hasty amplification of his own name and fame. Certainly his claim to an enduring reputation rests upon years of patient and skillful labor, not a few imprudent public performances by youngsters being "shown off."

Do not expect gratitude from your students, especially those to whom you have given extra time, energy, and fondest support. They will take you and your efforts for granted with rarely a word of thanks. (They may expect you to do everything for them. Perhaps this is good because it indicates that they have set you up on an idealized pedestal of perfection with all the time in the world to give to them and the willingness to do it also.) Like the ten lepers, one may return later to thank you for your efforts on his behalf. Remember, however, that when they, in turn, become teachers, they will repay you by giving themselves to *their* students, in accordance with the example you have set.

As a practical organizational aid, a sample student's work sheet is reproduced on the next page. Each teacher should revise and adapt the headings on the page to his own needs.

When using this method, the teacher will at some point, perhaps after Chapter 17 or 18, introduce outside materials to the student. Included will be works by various composers which are in the standard repertoire, and sections of other methods and manuals to give a well-rounded point of view and to encourage broad lines of growth. To facilitate the transitional phase, three lists of organ music are included in this chapter. Each is in approximate order of difficulty, beginning with very easy works:

    I. The organ works of J. S. Bach, except the *Orgelbüchlein*.

    II. The *Orgelbüchlein*, listed separately.

  III. After the student has become somewhat acquainted with the easier organ works of Bach, he should become familiar with the chorale preludes of Brahms. They should not, of course, be presented all at one time. One approximate order of presentation is indicated. There are other sequences which no doubt work out equally well.

■

    I. The organ works of J. S. Bach, except the *Orgelbüchlein*.

This sequence does not include all the organ works. It is partially an order of difficulty but, equally important, it is an order of approach to foster the development of an evolving and growing concept of Bach. But bear in mind that since all students are individuals with varying skills and needs, it is inadvisable to have an inflexible order of compositions through which all students must travel in the same identical order. This listing is therefore not arbitrary and is to be treated very freely. No student could possibly cover all the works listed below, or even a third of them; many omissions would be considered the normal rule for assignments. This author rarely uses certain of these works.

Roman numeral refers to volume number and Arabic numeral indicates page number in Peters Edition. (The Peters Edition is a good, inexpensive *Urtext*, but alto and tenor clefs are occasionally encountered; other editions are better for certain compositions, such as the "Eight Little Preludes and Fugues" and the *Orgelbüchlein*.)

Capital letter indicates major mode; lower-case letter signifies minor mode.

Two excerpts from Eight Little Preludes and Fugues:
    Fugue in a   VIII 67
    Fugue in G   VIII 61

Four compositions for manuals alone:
    Fughetta on Gottes Sohn ist kommen   V 22
    Allein Gott in der Höh' sei Ehr' VI 6
    Fughetta on Lob sei dem allmächtigen Gott   V 41
    Vater unser im Himmelreich V 51

Name	Margaret Teal	Class '65	Years piano 8

Name: Margaret Teal   Class '65   Years piano 8
Campus address: 210 Noble Hall   Major Church Music   Years organ 3
Campus phone: 505   B.A. ☐   B.Mus. ☑   Grade last semester B−
Church organ experience: One year assistant organist   Midterm grade B+
Directing experience: Junior choir, 6 months   Semester grade B+
Former teacher: Joseph Smith   Unexcused absences none

	9/25	10/2	10/9	10/16	10/23	10/30	11/2	11/6	11/13	11/15	11/20	11/21	11/27	12/4
BACH, Pre in D (IV 16)	S	✓	TM✓	(M)	M	M		M	M	R	—			
Instruction Book														
Chapter 22-Improvisation	✓			✓									✓	
BACH, Fugue in D		S	✓	✓	TM	(M)		M	M	R	—			
MESSIAEN, Majesté		S	(✓)	✓	✓	✓								
PEPPING, Vom Himmel		S	✓		✓		TM			M		M	M	
SCALES, on Piano		✓				✓							✓	
SWEELINCK, Fantasie			S	✓		✓			✓		✓			
PURCELL, Son. with 2 trumpets					S	✓					✓			
LANGLAIS, Epilogue							S	✓		✓	TM✓			
BRAHMS # 11									S	✓	✓			
BACH, Fan. in g									S	(✓)	✓			
BACH, Fugue in g										S	(✓)			

KEY	
S	Start work on this piece for next lesson
✓	Heard at lesson
(✓)	Discussed or partially played
TM	To memorize
(M)	Partially memorized
M	Played from memory
—	Dropped
R	Performed on student recital

In Dulci Jubilo IX 50
Fugue on Allein Gott in der Höh' sei Ehr' VI 30
Four excerpts from Eight Little Preludes and Fugues:
   Fugue in g VIII 64
   Prelude in e VIII 54
   Prelude in B♭ VIII 69
   Fugue in d VIII 52

Here begin the *Orgelbüchlein* (The Liturgical Year). (See list (II) for suggested order of presentation; do not cover the entire *Orgelbüchlein* at this point, but spread study of it out through at least the first half of this sequence.)

Four compositions for manuals alone:
   Kyrie, Gott heiliger Geist VII 28
   Fughetta on Allein Gott in der Höh' sei Ehr' VI 29
   Prelude in d III 42
   Wer nur den lieben Gott lässt walten (#53) V 56
Herzlich thut mich verlangen V 30
Pastorale I 88
Wo soll ich fliehen hin VII 84
Alla Breve VIII 72
Wenn wir in höchsten Nöten sein VII 74
Partita #2, O Gott du frommer Gott (the following partitas only: I, II, IV, V, VI, IX) (manuals alone) V 68-75
Canzona IV 58
Prelude and Fugue in e (The "Cathedral") III 88
Trio Sonata IV, first movement, Adagio-Vivace I 36
Wer nur den lieben Gott lässt walten VII 76
Prelude (only) in A II 14
Meine Seele erhebt den Herren (The Magnificat) VII 33
Prelude (only) in C III 62
Trio Sonata III, first movement, Andante I 24
Wachet auf, ruft uns die Stimme VII 72
Fantasia in c III 55
Ach bleib bei uns, Herr Jesu Christ VI 4
Prelude (only) in f II 29
Trio Sonata I, third movement, Allegro I 8
Nun freut euch, lieben Christen g'mein VII 36
Prelude and Fugue in C II 2
Von Gott will ich nicht lassen VII 70
Fantasia in G IV 62
Trio Sonata V, second movement, Largo I 54
Partita #3 (partita X only) V 88-90
Schmücke dich, o liebe Seele VII 50
Trio Sonata VI, second movement, Lento I 68
The "Little" Fugue in g IV 46
Trio Sonata IV, second movement, Andante I 39
Wir glauben all' an einen Gott, Schöpfer VII 78
Toccata (only) in d (The "Dorian") III 30
Valet will ich dir geben VII 56
Trio Sonata II, third movement, Allegro I 18
Fugue in c III 58
O Lamm Gottes, unschuldig VII 45
Prelude (only) in C II 46
Prelude and Fugue in a II 54
Kyrie, Gott heiliger Geist VII 23
Toccata and Fugue in d IV 27
Fugue on Meine Seele erhebt den Herren (The Magnificat) VII 29
Trio Sonata VI, first movement, Vivace I 63
Prelude (only) in c II 36
Komm, heiliger Geist, Herre Gott VII 4
Prelude and Fugue in b II 78

Concerto II, first movement (Vivaldi)   VIII 10
Jesus Christus, unser Heiland   VI 82
Trio Sonata I, first movement, Allegro Moderato   I 2
Fugue in G (The "Jig")   IX 4
Trio Sonata V, first movement, Allegro   I 46
Nun komm', der Heiden Heiland   VII 42
Prelude and Fugue in G   II 7
Kommst du nun, Jesu, vom Himmel herunter   VII 16
Toccata, Adagio and Fugue in C   III 84
Herr Jesu Christ, dich zu uns wend'   VI 70
Prelude in E♭   III 2
Fugue in E♭ ("St. Anne")   III 10
Canonic Variations on Vom Himmel hoch da komm ich her   V 92
Passacaglia and Fugue in c   I 76
Prelude and Fugue (The "Wedge") in e   II 64
Trio Sonata V, third movement, Allegro   I 58
An Wasserflüssen Babilone (double pedal)   VI 32
Fantasia and Fugue in g   II 20
Prelude and Fugue in D   IV 16
Toccata (only) in F   III 16

II. The *Orgelbüchlein*

This superb collection of 45 chorales seems to divide itself naturally into groups of five. Most students should be assigned all the items in group I in approximately that order, and then one or more from each of the succeeding groups as it is appropriate for their development. The order of groups is by no means inflexible, nor is the order of items within each group. These are not just good teaching materials: they are good for teaching because they are great music. Many are excellent for training in memorization. The Riemenschneider Edition is recommended; it is published by Oliver Ditson.

1. Easiest of the collection:

   #44 Alle Menschen müssen sterben
   #27 Christ lag in Todesbanden
    #6 Gelobet seist du, Jesu Christ
   #37 Vater unser im Himmelreich
   #34 Herr Jesu Christ, dich zu uns wend'

2. Mostly faster, louder: for developing coordination, facility, tempo, technique
   #11 Lobt Gott, ihr Christen, allzugleich
   #39 Es ist das Heil uns kommen her
    #3 Herr Christ, der ein'ge Gottes Sohn
    #8 Vom Himmel hoch, da komm' ich her
   #43 Wer nur den lieben Gott lässt walten

3. In minor, mostly softer: for developing artistry in phrasing, cultivation of a concept of melodic line
   #23 Da Jesus an dem Kreuze Stund
   #41 In dich hab' ich gehoffet, Herr
   #12 Jesu, meine Freude
   #45 Ach, wie flüchtig, ach wie nichtig
   #38 Durch Adams fall ist ganz verderbt

4. Ornaments. (Special note in reference to #40: assuming that the composer indicated the ornaments in the first half of this composition as a model or demonstration, the student should improvise or write in appropriate ornamentation in the second half in the same style.)
   #16   Das alte Jahr vergangen ist
   #40   Ich ruf' zu dir, Herr Jesu Christ
   #24   O Mensch, bewein' dein' Sünde gross
   #35a or #35b Liebster Jesu, wir sind hier
   #42   Wenn wir in höchsten Nöthen sein

5. For continuing development of technique. Various difficulties (fingering, pedaling, etc.) will be encountered.
   #18 Mit Fried' and Freud' ich fahr' dahin
   #30 Erstanden ist der heil'ge Christ
   #32 Heut' triumphiret Gottes Sohn
   #7 Der Tag, der ist so freudenreich
   #33 Komm, Gott Schöpfer, heiliger Geist

6. For devoting attention to concepts in registration.
   #2 Gottes Sohn ist kommen
   #9 Vom Himmel kam der Engel Schaar
   #22 Christus, der uns selig macht
   #28 Jesus Christus, unser Heiland
   #15 Helft mir Gott's Güte preisen

7. For "thumbing down." These may be played with one hand on two manuals simultaneously, for the purpose of bringing out a melody, clarifying counterpoint, or controlling registration of the alto voice.
   #19 Herr Gott, nun schleuss den Himmel auf
   #13 Christum wir sollen loben schon
   #20 O Lamm Gottes, unschuldig
   #26 Hilf Gott, dass mir's gelinge
   #21 Christe, du Lamm Gottes

8. For interpretation, registration, drill in rhythmic problems.
   #31 Erschienen ist der herrlich' Tag
   #5 Puer Natus in Bethlehem
   #4 Lob sei dem allmächtigen Gott
   #25 Wir danken dir, Herr Jesu Christ
   #1 Nun komm, der Heiden Heiland

9. More difficult:
   #14 Wir Christen-leut'
   #36 Dies sind die heil'gen zehn Gebot'
   #17 In dir ist Freude
   #29 Christ ist erstanden
   #10 In dulci jubilo

III. From Chorale Preludes, Op. 122, of Johannes Brahms (The E. Power Biggs edition is recommended; it is published by Mercury Music Corporation):
   #6b O wie selig seid ihr doch, ihr Frommen
   #8a Es ist ein Ros' entsprungen
   #2 Herzliebster Jesu
   #11 O Welt, ich muss dich lassen (II)
   #9 Herzlich tut mich verlangen (I)
   #5a Schmücke dich, o liebe Seele
   #10 Herzlich tut mich verlangen (II)
   #3 O Welt, ich muss dich lassen (I)
   #7 O Gott, du frommer Gott
   #1 Mein Jesu, der du mich

This Instruction Book was completed in the year of our Lord 1964, and it is dedicated to His glory.

Special thanks are due my wife, Margaret, whose support and encouragement were the inspiration for this book. I express also my gratitude to Miss Ruth Olson and other members of the staff of Augsburg Publishing House for valuable aid.

This book is intended for all the persons I have known, and especially for all whom I have loved; and it is further intended for those whom I have not known who have spent any time in the contemplation of beauty. We organists have a responsibility to God and to man, to explore the aesthetic grandeur, the poignant intimacy, and the nobility which are the organ's unique province; and I can only hope that this book contributes a few notes to the unending stream of beauty which surrounds us in this life, and which must surely be an intimation of the hymns of joy and holy ecstasy which shall be heard, through His grace, in the next.